The Christian Man

Written by

C. A. Brewer
P. D. Buford
R. M. Buie

R. M Davis
D. A. Lewis
Dan Segraves

This book is designed for personal or group study.

PENTECOSTAL PUBLISHING HOUSE
8855 DUNN ROAD
HAZELWOOD, MO 63042-2299

Word Aflame Elective Series

Family Life Selections

The Christian Youth
The Christian Woman
The Christian Man
The Christian Parent

Other Elective Series Volumes

WHY? A Study of Christian Standards
Spiritual Growth and Maturity
Bible Doctrines–Foundation of the Church
Salvation–Key to Eternal Life
The Bible–It's Origin and Use
Strategy for Life for Singles and Young Adults
Spiritual Leadership/Successful Soulwinning
Your New Life
Friendship, Courtship, and Marriage
Purpose at Sunset
Values That Last
Meet the United Pentecostal Church International
Facing the Issues
The Holy Spirit
Life's Choices

EDITORIAL STAFF

R. M. Davis .... Editor
P. D. Buford .... Associate Editor

J. L. Hall .... Editor in Chief
United Pentecostal Church International

©1990 by the Pentecostal Publishing House, Hazelwood, Missouri. All rights reserved.
Reprint History: 1995, 1998
ISBN 1-56722-033-9

CURRICULUM COMMITTEE: James E. Boatman, P. D. Buford, Dan Butler, R. M. Davis, J. L. Hall, G. W. Hassebrock, Garth E. Hatheway, E. E. Jolley, Vernon McGarvey, Chester L. Mitchell, Ronald Nation, David L. Reynolds, Charles A. Rutter, R. L. Wyser.

Foreword

P. D. Buford
Associate Editor
Word Aflame Publications

Everyone needs a man. Little girls need a man to love and nurture them, to train and cherish them, to show them how special they really are, and for them to call "Daddy."

Little boys need a man to be a role model for them, to show them how real men treat others, to never be too busy to be a friend, to never say, "Do as I say, not as I do," and for them to call "Dad."

Women need a man to love and cherish them, to provide for them, to give them a strong root note with which to harmonize their lives, to offer them a strong, stable relationship in which to travel life's road, and for them to call "Husband."

Men need a man to be their teacher, their leader, to be their comrade, to be their mentor, to give them balance and to be their sounding board, and for them to call "Brother."

Less fortunate people need a man to lean on, to offer them counsel and encouragement, to help them up when they stumble, to show them that down does not mean out, and for them to call "Friend."

Everyone needs a man. Goliath called to Israel, "Give me a man, that we may fight together" (I Samuel 17:10). Even an evil adversary needs a man, for without a man to conquer, he cannot be a victor.

Everyone needs a man. The lame man at the pool of Bethesda responded to Jesus' question "Wilt thou be made whole?" with these words: "Sir, I have no man, when the water is troubled, to put me into the pool"(John 5:7).

Everyone needs a man. The prophet Ezekiel said, "And I sought for a man among them, that should make up the hedge, and stand in the gap before me for the land, that I should not destroy it: but I found none"(Ezekiel 22:30).

Everyone needs a man. God Himself even felt this need, "So God created man in his own image, in the image of God created he him"(Genesis 1:27).

I needed a man in my life. God gave to me many and varied men—some I call "Friend," some I call "Teacher," some I call "Pastor," some I call "Brother," but the greatest I call "Dad."

Many godly men have walked across the impressionable soil of my soul, but Dad's footprints remain cleaner, purer, more steadfast, and more Christ-like than any man I know. Perhaps it is because of Christ whom he follows faithfully.

It is our desire that this book, *The Christian Man*, written by Christian men, will serve to hold up a light that all may see the way of Christian manhood. After all, everyone needs a man.

Contents

Chapter	Page
Foreword	3
1. Leadership—How Far?	7
2. Mixing Career and Family	18
3. On Being a Man	30
4. Spirituality and Christian Service	42
5. Remaking Broken Vessels	54
6. The Responsibility of Fatherhood	65
7. Teaching Principles and Standards to Children	75
8. Marriage—I Found a Good Thing	91
9. Morality—Take the High Road	103
10. Be the Best You Can Be	115
11. Here I Stand	125
12. The Golden Rule (Relationships)	137
13. Bloom Where You Are Planted	149

Leadership—How Far? 1

Watch ye, stand fast in the faith, quit you like men, be strong. Let all your things be done with charity.
I Corinthians 16:13-14

Start With the Scriptures

Matthew 7:9-12
II Corinthians 10:8
Ephesians 5:25-33; 6:4, 9
Colossians 3:21
I Timothy 3:1-12
James 5:4
I Peter 3:7; 5:2-3

While men and women are equal before God, they do have diverse roles and responsibilities. (See, for example, Galatians 3:28; I Corinthians 11:3; and Ephesians 5:22-25.)

One of the greatest causes of marital difficulty is the confusion of this divinely ordained plan. Marriage is God's idea (Genesis 2:18-24). He intended for marriage to be a blessed, rewarding experience for both the husband and wife, not the bitter, frustrating trial it sometimes is for some people.

The Bible teaches that the husband should assume certain leadership responsibilities; however, these responsibilities are often misunderstood, neglected, or distorted. If we can obtain a clear understanding of the Word of God on the subject of leadership in the home and make a commitment to following divine instructions, we will immensely enhance the success of marriages and family relationships.

Loving Leadership

"Watch ye, stand fast in the faith, quit you like men, be strong. Let all your things be done with charity" (I Corinthians 16:13-14).

Paul offered four major points as qualifications for leadership that equally apply to a husband.

Alertness. A man should be alert, especially to the spiritual dangers which threaten his home and family. He should have the foresight to see where present trends and actions will ultimately lead (Proverbs 27:12). He must accept the responsibility for protecting his family spiritually, emotionally, and physically.

Firmness in Faith. A man's leadership involves his example of faith. Perhaps we could understand this in a twofold manner: ❶ A man should adhere firmly to the truth, and ❷ he should be a man of unswerving faith (belief, confidence in God).

There are many voices of skepticism and false teaching; so a wife and children must see in their husband and father a steady illustration of faith and truth.

Strength. Manhood and moral weakness are antithetical. While the warped values of a godless society tend to stress visible and physical accomplishments, like the overt physical strength of body-building, the Word of God emphasizes the inner strengths which endure.

The strength desired in a man of God is that

described by Paul: "Be strong in the Lord, and in the power of his might" (Ephesians 6:10). This is the strength which enables a person to "stand against the wiles of the devil" (Ephesians 6:11).

Love. Love should be a great concern for men. All of a man's qualities—his alertness, his faith, his strength—must be tempered by love. If not, his alertness may turn to harsh judgmentalism, his faith to hypocritical superiority, and his strength to brutal force.

A man's leadership must constantly be guided by love for God and for his family. The kind of love needed is described in I Corinthians 13:4-7.

- Love is longsuffering.
- Love is kind.
- Love does not envy.
- Love does not exalt itself.
- Love is not puffed up.
- Love behaves properly.
- Love is not self-centered.
- Love is not short tempered.
- Love thinks no evil.
- Love rejoices in truth.
- Love bears all things.
- Love believes all things.
- Love hopes all things.
- Love endures all things.

These fourteen qualities should be the basis of what a man does in his leadership role.

The enemy will, of course, tempt a man to pervert his leadership responsibilities by failing to meet the demands of love. A man will be tempted to:

- Be impatient.
- Be unkind.
- Envy.
- Promote himself.
- Be puffed up.
- Behave improperly.

- Be self-centered.
- Be short tempered.
- Think evil.
- Rejoice in iniquity.
- Be intolerant.
- Be skeptical.
- Be hopeless.
- Reject unpleasant responsibilities.

A Man's Example

There can be no better example of the proper handling of a man's leadership responsibilities than that offered by the Lord Jesus in His relationship with the church: "Husbands, love your wives, even as Christ also loved the church, and gave himself for it. . . . So ought men to love their wives as their own bodies. He that loveth his wife loveth himself. For no man ever yet hated his own flesh; but nourisheth and cherisheth it, even as the Lord the church: For we are members of his body, of his flesh, and of his bones. For this cause shall a man leave his father and mother, and shall be joined unto his wife, and they two shall be one flesh. . . . let every one of you in particular so love his wife even as himself" (Ephesians 5:25, 28-33).

The example of the Lord illustrates well the importance of doing all of one's things with charity (love). In the process of giving Himself for the church and daily nourishing and cherishing the church, Jesus fulfilled and continues to fulfill all of the fourteen characteristics of genuine love.

Unhindered Prayer

In a passage discussing the husband-wife relationship, Peter wrote, "Likewise, ye husbands, dwell with them according to knowledge, giving honour unto the wife, as unto the weaker vessel, and as being heirs together of the grace of life; that your prayers be not hindered" (I Peter 3:7).

It is important to note that men are to dwell with their wives *according to knowledge*. That is, the matter of the treatment of one's wife is worthy of a great deal of consideration, contemplation, and study. It is not to be approached lightly or irreverently. One reason for such carefulness is that the marriage relationship symbolizes the relationship between Christ and the church.

The husband is to honor his wife as a fragile (weaker) vessel. He should not treat her like a waste basket, but like an expensive vase!

Another reason for considerate, kind, thoughtful treatment is that God has ordained that a husband and wife be heirs *together* of the grace of life. When they take the vows of marriage, they are no longer two; they are one flesh.

"For this cause shall a man leave his father and mother, and shall be joined unto his wife, and they two shall be one flesh" (Ephesians 5:31). This verse, which originally appeared in Genesis 2:24, is repeated three times in the New Testament and is obviously the original and basic purpose and intent of God in marriage.

With marriage, a new family structure is formed. While a man will continue to honor his parents, he is now the head of his own family. In the strictest sense, he is no longer the person he once was. He has now assumed a new identity, and that identity includes his wife. He cannot be considered singly and alone any more; he is now an heir of the grace (gift) of life *together* with someone else.

A third reason that it is important that a husband have the right relationship with his wife is that their prayers will not be hindered. In other words, a man's relationship with God is influenced by his relationship with his wife. Since a man's identity now includes his wife, he can no more neglect her than he can neglect himself (Ephesians 5:28-29) if he hopes to be properly related to God.

The Purpose for Authority

Unregenerate men tend to think of authority in terms of oppression. Those who have authority are sorely tempted to use it for personal gain, even if it means abusing those beneath them. Those who are under authority tend to think of it in negative terms and to always be suspicious of their superiors.

But Paul revealed the proper purpose for authority: "For though I should boast somewhat more of our authority, which the Lord hath given us for edification, and not for your destruction, I should not be ashamed" (II Corinthians 10:8).

The Lord gives authority for edification, not destruction. Edification speaks of building up, encouraging, and strengthening. Therefore, the Lord gives men authority so that they can build up, encourage, and strengthen those for whom they are responsible. This is true even in a man's relationship with his children: "And, ye fathers, provoke not your children to wrath: but bring them up in the nurture and admonition of the Lord" (Ephesians 6:4). "Fathers, provoke not your children to anger, lest they be discouraged" (Colossians 3:21).

The Golden Rule

The Golden Rule applies to the home as well as other areas of life. The husband must not violate this sacred rule of conduct. One interesting aspect often overlooked about the Golden Rule is that it was given in the context of a father's relationship with his children.

"Or what man is there of you, whom if his son ask bread, will he give him a stone? Or if he ask a fish, will he give him a serpent? If ye then, being evil, know how to give good gifts unto your children, how much more shall your Father which is in heaven give good things to them that ask him? Therefore all things whatsoever ye would that men should do to you, do ye even so to them: for this is the law and the prophets" (Matthew 7:9-12).

A man's leadership in his family should constantly be influenced by a silent question: *"How would I want to be treated?"*

"Would I want to be spoken to harshly?"

"Would I want someone to refuse to listen to me?"

"Would I want to be ridiculed?"

In the final analysis, there is not a great deal of mystery in how a man should lead—he should lead in the way he would want to be led.

Requirements for Spiritual Leadership

Paul listed for Timothy the specific requirements for bishops (pastors) and deacons. While only those who are called of God to these ministries should aspire to them, the standard of leadership is seen at its highest development. Although all men are not bishops or deacons, they would do well to hold these standards as the goal toward which they reach. (See I Timothy 3:1-12.) These guidelines include:

- Righting all wrong (blamelessness).
- Moral purity (husband of one wife).
- Vigilance (alertness against evil).
- Sobriety (sound mindedness).
- Good behavior (a characteristic of love).
- Hospitality (an interest in others).
- Ability to teach (even if it is only his family, and mostly by example).
- Abstinence (from addictive habits).

- Non-violent (no striker).
- Generosity (not greedy).
- Patience (a characteristic of love).
- Self-control (no brawler).
- No covetousness.
- Excellence in family relationships.
- No pride.
- A good reputation.
- Steadfastness in the faith.

A careful comparison of these characteristics with those of love (I Corinthians 13) and the requirements for manhood (I Corinthians 16:13-14) reveals remarkable similarities.

Leadership at Large

While leadership is inherent in a man's relationship with his family, many men find themselves thrust into leadership roles in the business world or in the church. The Bible does not neglect the man's responsibilities in these situations. While a great deal is written about the responsibilities of servants, the masters are also addressed: "And, ye masters, do the same things unto them, forbearing threatening: knowing that your Master also is in heaven; neither is there respect of persons with him" (Ephesians 6:9).

Men in positions of authority and leadership should be as thoughtful and considerate of those under them as employees are expected to be of their employers. No use should be made of threats. By implication, there should be no abuse, mentally, physically, or economically.

No matter how highly placed a person is in leadership, he should remember he too has a Master in heaven, and that Master is no respecter of persons. God will someday judge all men, and His judgment will be untainted.

The law of Moses addressed the just treatment of workers. Even the New Testament reveals the concern God has for those who are abused by oppressive masters: "Behold, the hire of the labourers who have reaped down your fields, which is of you kept back by fraud, crieth: and the cries of them which have reaped are entered into the ears of the Lord of sabaoth" (James 5:4).

God will judge those who fail to keep their agreements with those who work for them. Vengeance belongs to God (Romans 12:19). Employers and managers must not in any way defraud those for whom they are responsible.

Eric Hoffer wrongly suggested, "Charlatanism is to some degree indispensable to effective leadership." On the contrary, the Bible declares that leaders must be transparent and honest.

To those in spiritual leadership in the church, Peter wrote, "Feed the flock of God which is among you, taking the oversight thereof, not by constraint, but willingly; not for filthy lucre, but of a ready mind; neither as being lords over God's heritage, but being ensamples to the flock" (I Peter 5:2-3).

Spiritual leadership is seen here as a feeding process. It is, again, a relationship of edification, encouragement, and upbuilding. It is not to be assumed out of a mere sense of duty, but willingly. It must not be assumed in hopes of money, but because one believes God has called him. The spiritual leader must not see himself as a "lord" or master over something that belongs to God; he must instead see himself as an example for others to follow.

Leadership Summarized

Contrary to the world's opinion of a leader as a manipulator or dictator, the Bible pictures him as a loving father who leads by word, deed, and example. He may teach, but the value of his teaching will grow out of his prior illustration in his own life of the principles he teaches.

A man must lead as Jesus led. He willingly gave Himself for those He led. A man must recognize that manhood has to do not with physical prowess but with alertness, faith, moral strength, and love. A Christian man understands love as defined in I Corinthians 13 and not as the twisted concept of love portrayed by secular movies and television shows. He should attempt to measure up to the standard of manhood and leadership required of bishops and deacons.

Most of all, a man must use his authority, whether at home, in the church, or on the job, not to destroy or hurt but to encourage, strengthen, and build up those for whom he is responsible.

Test Your Knowledge

1. What are the four characteristics of manhood?
2. List six characteristics of love.
3. Why will prayers be hindered if a husband and wife do not have the right relationship?
4. What is the purpose of authority?
5. In what context was the Golden Rule given?
6. List five qualifications for a bishop or deacon.

Apply Your Knowledge

List the fourteen characteristics of love on an index card. Carry it with you for two weeks. Each day, prayerfully ask God to show you how you can improve your leadership by better exercising one specific characteristic of love.

Each day in prayer ask God to help you to behave like a man, to be alert, to stand fast in the faith, to be strong, and to do all things with charity.

Ask your wife to write on an index card the one thing she would most like to see happen in your relationship. Take the card and prayerfully seek a specific way to make that thing happen.

Ask your children to write on an index card the one thing they would like most to see happen in their relationship with you. Take the cards and prayerfully seek specific ways to make those things happen.

At the end of two weeks, take some time with the Lord to list the specific things you did to encourage, strengthen, and build up your family. What was their response to your efforts?

Expand Your Knowledge

Every day for two weeks, read I Corinthians 16:13-14, I Corinthians 13:4-7 and Ephesians 5:25-33; 6:4. Read these passages slowly and carefully, meditating on how you could fulfill them in your relationships.

Obtain and study a book such as *Maximized Manhood: A Guide to Family Survival* by Edwin Louis Cole (Springdale, PA: Whitaker House, 1982) and *If Only He Knew* by Gary Smalley (Grand Rapids, MI: Zondervan, 1982).

2. Mixing Career and Family

> *By faith Noah, being warned of God of things not seen as yet, moved with fear, prepared an ark to the saving of his house; by the which he condemned the world, and became heir of the righteousness which is by faith.*
>
> Hebrews 11:7

Start With the Scriptures

Genesis 6:5–7:1
Acts 18:3
I Corinthians 3:9-23
Hebrews 11:7

The dramatic events of Noah's life and his personal submission to God's plan have long been wonderful examples to Christians. His life has also been a great inspiration to those who struggle with complete obedience to God's will. But Noah's life is not simply a one-dimensional object lesson in faith. It contains many useful lessons for everyday living, not the least of which is a practical demonstration of a righteous man successfully mixing "career" with family responsibilities.

Building the ark was a gigantic undertaking that required great physical labor. Year after year, the job demanded Noah's daily attention. His task was not easy. The demands of building had to be satisfied while he simultaneously fulfilled his responsibilities as head of his household, spiritual leader, husband, and father.

Very much like Christian men today, Noah experienced the personal anxiety associated with balancing the forces of career and family. But in spite of daily pressures, he successfully completed the ark that brought salvation to his family.

In today's world, time dedicated to a career does not span one hundred twenty years (although it may certainly seem like it at times). At the same time, the working man must deal with the increasing demands on his time. A Christian man should be as successful as Noah was in properly balancing career and family relationships because the rewards are as great—the saving of his household.

The complex task is by no means easy, however, for it demands extra efforts to achieve a genuine compatibility between career demands and family needs.

Career Is the Will of God

In the same manner that God communicated His divine plan for Noah's labor, He reveals an ordained plan for each husband to provide adequately for his family. This is especially true for the believer. The apostle Paul addressed the issue in certain terms. "But if any provide not for his own, and specially for those of his own house, he hath denied the faith, and is worse than an infidel" (I Timothy 5:8).

This instruction to the New Testament church expresses God's charge to every Christian husband—that he fulfill his responsibilities to provide for his own house. If, as family leaders, we fail to meet this obligation, our actions will be judged as those of the unbeliever (infidel). The Christian husband must insure that his family is provided with adequate food, clothing, and shelter. Hard times and difficult employers may come, but he must cope with these adversities.

Illness or injury that prevents employment are unpredictable facts of life, but no husband should be guilty of laziness and idleness. Irresponsibility brings great personal reproach and severely limits the influence of a husband's Christian testimony.

Within the limits of his God-given abilities, a husband should pursue a career that will provide for the basic needs of his family. The Scriptures teach, "For unto whomsoever much is given, of him shall be much required" (Luke 12:48).

Just as individual talents and abilities differ, our social, economic, and educational backgrounds also vary. Because of this, individuals should not be tempted to make unfair comparisons between themselves and others. It is really unimportant what type of employment a person has as long as it is honest and godly. In both spiritual and natural efforts, the critical question is, "Are we doing our very best for our family and our Lord?"

During His temptation by the devil, Jesus provided insights into man's earthly labors. He said, "Man shall not live by bread alone, but by every word of God" (Luke 4:4). Just as it is impossible for anyone to live spiritually by natural nourishment alone, it is equally impossible for men and women to spiritually mature in God when material and financial resources are completely consumed for personal, and often selfish reasons.

From the increase of our labor, we are to offer tithes and offerings unto the Lord (Malachi 3:7-12). Again Noah's example teaches us this biblical principle. When God delivered Noah's family by the ark, Noah's first act after leaving it was to build an altar and offer burnt-offerings unto the Lord (Genesis 8:20). In a similar manner, a generous portion of our earnings should go directly as an offering to the Lord and to support His church. It is an offering not to be given grudgingly but freely in thanksgiving for God's blessing on our labors.

As the believer is blessed with material gain and advancement, he is to offer firstfruits as a sacrifice before the Lord by giving of his tithes and offerings. The Christian is challenged by the Scriptures to prove God in this area and see if He will not pour out such an immense blessing that it cannot be received (Malachi 3:10). There is a corresponding warning that if tithes and offerings are withheld from God through selfishness or ingratitude, such action is the same as robbing God, and in turn, He will not bless our efforts.

As each man pursues his given career and provides appropriately for his family, he must not neglect his responsibility to the church and its financial needs. By stubbornly closing our fists and refusing to give into God's storehouse, we shut off one of the greatest sources of personal blessing and spiritual growth that is available to us.

Career and God

In every aspect of life, God desires that all our efforts be blessed. Our chosen occupation or career is no exception. As God seeks men to serve Him, He consistently calls men with natural initiative, enthusiasm, and ambition whose character is tempered with true humility.

A popular slogan says, "Be all you can be!" It is not God's will that Christian men just "get by" on the job or barely achieve or perform below average levels in their chosen field. Instead, He desires that they excel in all they do because of His touch and presence in their lives. When men set their goals high, strive to be their very best, and render to God that which is His, He will bless them in their business and career endeavors.

At the same time, the career-minded man must insure that his feet are planted firmly on the ground, both spiritually and naturally. He must not question so much whether his goals are too high or a given profession is beyond his reach, but he must honestly ask himself if he has given God's will preeminence in the selection of his career. Certainly, there are some careers which are based on carnal values that are totally alien to sound Christian principles. As a child of God, we must have the spiritual sensitivity and willingness to seek God's direction in considering an appropriate profession. Those career fields which adversely influence our walk with God, weaken our testimony, or detract from our faithfulness must not be pursued.

Career and Family

It can be readily shown that the goals of Noah's career and those of his family were identical. Through the building of the ark, Noah insured the salvation of his family. In other words, his career and family objectives were in harmony. This is a key characteristic of a properly balanced career and family perspective. Much of the agonizing frustration suffered by families could be avoided if this "harmony" principle were applied to their career and family interactions. A career opportunity should not be pursued in isolation without regard for its effect on family relationships. All family members need to sense that they are loved and are an important part of the family unit before their support of a career can be strong and sincere.

Families should feel so comfortable with the husband or father's job that they are able to share equally in both his victories and defeats. If they are, they will be his greatest supporters. On the other hand, if family members become jealous or bitter of time spent at work or in the office, the stability of the family becomes threatened and may seriously endanger the family unit.

A Case in Point

As Bob Jones talked about the deteriorating relationship between his career and family, a deep frustration came through in his voice. "The rat race at work has completely overwhelmed me. There used to be days when I could stop and breathe and maybe smell the roses as they say, but now, it's just impossible. There's scarcely enough time in the day to make a living, much less spend time with my wife and children."

Bob's words have a very familiar ring to them. He is not unlike many hard-working men trying their best to succeed in a very competitive world. Bob is typical. He is a successful insurance salesman with a large clientele in a metropolitan area. An average day goes something like this:

The day begins at 5:00 a.m. with a quick cup of coffee and a frustrating drive through heavy traffic to the office. The first hour is spent reviewing paperwork generated from policies written over the last week.

The rest of the morning is consumed with an endless number of telephone calls, both made and received, with current and potential customers. Lunch consists of cheese crackers, a diet Coke, and more telephone calls. In the afternoon, the boss conducts a pressure-packed review of Bob's sales performance and efficiency rating for the quarter.

All through the day, Bob makes appointments with customers for the evening hours. At 6:00 p.m., he drives up to the window of a fast-food chain, orders a hamburger, and prepares for his first appointment at 6:30. By 10:30 p.m., the appointments are finished. He slumps behind the wheel of his car and begins the forty-five minute drive home.

It is after midnight as he quietly eases into bed. He's totally exhausted. His wife and children were asleep long ago. As he glances at his resting wife, he realizes it is already tomorrow and his next work day begins in less than five hours.

Sadly, Bob has no idea what kind of day his family has had. Was it good, bad, or average? Did the children behave? How are they doing in school? He has had no opportunity to ask those questions in weeks. And Bob's life is not as unusual as we might imagine.

While no two men have exactly the same kind of job pressures, the rapid pace and intensity of today's business environment is all too familiar to many of them. The increasing cost of living and rising financial obligations are requiring the working man to devote more and more of his time to earning a living.

In some cases, it is not unusual for men, after finishing a full day's work at one job, to go immediately to another job in order to earn sufficient income. In many family situations, the heavy financial load of modern life has dictated that the wife enter the work force in order to "make ends meet." Where does this place the family and home in the order of things? Most likely, not at the top.

The Christian man must also struggle with the same career demands, financial strains, and personal anxieties. The child of God may not be *of* this world, but he surely is *in* this high-speed, "winner-take-all" world. His challenge is to bring harmony to the opposing priorities of career and family while still fulfilling his responsibilities to God and church.

The quotation below is representative of an increasing number of Christian men who are concerned about the detrimental clash of priorities.

"I feel a little like a circus juggler. All my obligations are in the air at the same time—career, family, church, and community! Each one requires my individual attention so that none are accidentally dropped. It's a nerve-racking balancing act. Can anybody help me?"

Three Principles for Priority

On our own, finding the perfect balance for all these demands is extremely difficult. However, with a positive attitude and uncompromising faith that God helps us, the task can be accomplished. Faith and hope are essential. Noah had both. Combining a positive outlook with a dynamic faith, he accomplished the miraculous. Because God is no respecter of persons, every believer has that same "measure of faith" (Romans 12:3).

Armed with faith, we can find answers in the Word of God. God's truths are always there, and we believe them, but we often have difficulty applying them to our specific circumstances. Three valuable principles from the Scriptures are particularly helpful in solving the "balancing act" of career and family.

Avail yourself of God's advice. Use the power of prayer to seek out God's counsel. Jesus said it best: "Seek ye first the kingdom of God . . . and all these things shall be added unto you" (Matthew 6:33). In other words, put first things first.

The first priority is a genuine relationship with God. When this is done, all other things (job, possessions, and reputation) will fit surprisingly into place because we gave Him first priority. Sure it takes effort to pray; anything worthwhile does. But in God's presence there is never a wasted moment.

Keep in mind that whatever activity we give time to is what we consider most important. Time spent in communion with God will produce real answers to those critical job and family decisions that previously were completely out of reach. It is *through* Christ that we are able to do all things (Philippians 4:13). Without Him, there is not much hope.

Avoid the extreme or excessive. "Let your moderation be known unto all men" (Philippians 4:5).

The use of moderation in all aspects of career and family relationships will place these competing elements in proper perspective. By making moderation the centerpiece for actions in the workplace and at home, any tendency to the extreme can be avoided. For example, the "workaholic" never experiences real satisfaction and peace because of his inconsiderate and excessive commitment to his work. Instead of placing work in proper perspective, work for work's sake becomes his god.

The other extreme is equally wrong. The man who habitually shirks his responsibility to provide for his family is consumed with his self-centered desires to the detriment of family need. It is through moderation that we learn to temper our actions by careful consideration of their consequences to others.

It should come as no surprise then that temperance (to demonstrate restraint or moderation in action, thought, appetites, or passions) is listed among the fruit of the Spirit in the life of the Christian (Galatians 5:23). Temperance is not compromise; rather it is the avoidance of the extravagant or extreme.

Learning to leave our work *at* work and family issues *at* home is not only a practical application of the principle of moderation, but will significantly reduce the frustration levels of all concerned. By evaluating our personal behavior patterns we can assess whether or not our daily actions reflect a temperate, controlled response. Extreme or excessive behavior and actions will not resolve family conflicts, only worsen them.

Always choose people over things. Sometimes tough decisions are unavoidable when career and family goals are incompatible. This is dramatically seen in the large number of "working wives" today. Somehow we have convinced ourselves that the times require the wife to work in order to sustain a reasonable standard of living. And certainly there are cases where, due to need, it is necessary. However, in many households, the wife's income is expended primarily on nonessential goods or services. Households with two working spouses tend to quickly become dependent upon the wife's income to meet additional financial commitments and debts. This extra income, however, cannot adequately compensate for the absence of a wife and mother from the home.

If a husband elects to lower his family's lifestyle somewhat or eliminate purchases of luxury items so that his wife can remain at home, it is an honorable sacrifice in light of the many benefits of her presence there. When families determine to live within the standard of living provided for by the father alone, they are following God's order for the home. Such personal courage adds a new dimension to Jesus' words, "If any man will come after me, let him deny himself, and take up his cross, and follow me" (Matthew 16:24).

When the family's welfare and spiritual well-being are truly endangered by the most successful of careers, the career must adapt to the family. Things soon corrupt and rust, but the spiritual condition of the Christian man and his family have eternal meaning and value.

As Christian men, our relationship to God and to the family is of utmost importance. The mixing of career and family schedules and priorities in such a manner as to protect these meaningful relationships will continue to be a difficult challenge to every working man. Conflicts will arise between the demands of the workplace (increased hours, better pay, and added prestige or position) and the emotional and spiritual needs of the family unit. These competing purposes can be resolved through personal prayer, applying moderation in all things, and by deciding issues, not on the basis of career and financial gain alone, but with the family's spiritual best interest as the chief concern.

Test Your Knowledge

1. In today's society, why is it so difficult to successfully "mix" career and family?
2. What are the consequences of the Christian man's failure to properly provide for his family?
3. Does God expect the Christian man to excel in his career or occupation?
4. What types of careers or jobs should not be pursued by the Christian man?
5. When family members become bitter and jealous of career demands, what are the results?
6. Why are Christian men finding it more and more difficult to cope with the "balancing act" of career and family?
7. Why is prayer such a vital tool for resolving career and family conflicts?
8. List the three principles for priority.

Apply Your Knowledge

Career, family, and church activities are often in conflict. What have you done or do you plan to do to resolve these conflicts in your life? What career choices are you making or have you made that enrich family relationships?

In the everyday activities of your career, lifestyle, or family atmosphere, are the principles of moderation and temperance being applied? Examine the interactions between your career and family goals. Determine if you are applying biblical principles to reduce conflicts and incompatibilities.

Expand Your Knowledge

If you are just entering the work place, research the possible job fields and occupations in which you have interest. Compare these to your personal family goals. Make an appointment with your pastor to discuss the advantages and disadvantages of pursuing specific careers and their impact on family life. Listen carefully to his perspective and counsel.

If you are a veteran of the work place, evaluate the impact of your job on family, church, and community activities. If married, discuss with your spouse particular job pressures you are experiencing. Find solutions together.

3. On Being A Man

Watch ye, stand fast in the faith, quit you like men, be strong.

I Corinthians 16:13

Start With the Scriptures

Psalm 8:4-5; 139:14
Proverbs 16:32; 23:7
Ecclesiastes 12:13
Matthew 6:33

Acts 28:7
Romans 12:3
Philippians 1:27
II Timothy 4:6-8

A crowning achievement for a male is to be a God-fearing man. An individual can physically be a male but not necessarily be a "man." Being a God-fearing man involves character and other qualities that a male does not automatically possess.

The old adage, "The only difference between men and boys is the price of their toys," is only partly true. There is a dividing line between men and boys that each boy should desire to cross. Being a man is an honorable goal for a boy—not a sissy, a wimp or a push-over; not a dunce or a dude; not a ladies' man or a mamma's boy; not a superman body with a playboy brain, but a God-fearing man. Nothing in all of God's creation will take the place of a God-fearing man.

In this chapter we will be speaking of a God-fearing man but will simply use the word *man*. The thought is that a true man will fear God and hate evil.

On the sixth day of creation God created man and woman. This was His masterpiece, His concluding work of creation. Man was made to have dominion over all of God's other creation, being superior in so many ways. Because of man's abilities, he can conquer and dominate a brute beast that has more physical strength than he has. Mankind is the most precious stone in God's crown of creation.

David made an interesting observation which at first glance appears to border on bragging. Instead, though, it is simply an honest statement of fact that needs to be brought to the awareness of all men. "I will praise thee; for I am fearfully and wonderfully made: marvellous are thy works; and that my soul knoweth right well"(Psalm 139:14).

Man is fearfully and wonderfully made. It is amazing how the human body functions, moves, repairs itself, thinks, reasons, and believes. God's works are awesome and marvelous, and we can be deeply aware of this. It is not the height of vanity to think that we are special in God's eyes. This is the position for which God has designed us.

Before the Fall, man had a unique fellowship with God. The created and the Creator communed each evening. This closeness came to an end when sin entered and separated man from God. Thanks to God's provision, through the new birth experience man can again enjoy that close fellowship with his

Creator. This remarkable fellowship is yet another statement of mankind's uniqueness.

For a man to reach his maximum potential, though, he should always remember his frailties. Man should not think of himself more highly than he ought to think (Romans 12:3).

In realizing that we are the highest of all of God's creation, a person needs to keep his view of himself in proper perspective. Our self-esteem and self-confidence should never overcome our understanding of our rightful place. David asked a probing question: "What is man, that thou art mindful of him? . . . For thou hast made him a little lower than the angels" (Psalm 8:4-5).

Will Rogers, the cowboy humorist, took David's question a step further and said that "God made man a little lower than the angels, and he has been getting a little lower ever since." Although mankind is special and set apart from all the rest of God's creation, it is still astounding that God would be mindful and considerate of us.

Man needs to possess two seemingly contradictory attributes—a healthy self-esteem and a healthy humility. As impossible as this may seem, God desires that we strive to obtain this remarkable mixture.

In order to build strong families, strong churches, strong cities, and nations, God needs men. They are the foundational building blocks of stability and leadership for which God reaches.

Josiah Gilbert Holland, in *Wanted,* wrote an appeal for men.

> "God give us men. A time like this demands strong minds, great hearts, true faith and ready hands!
>
> "Men whom the lust of office does not kill,
>
> "Men whom the spoils of office cannot buy,

"Men who possess opinions and a will,
"Men who love honor, men who cannot lie."

Paul, in writing to the Corinthians, gave some excellent admonitions. "Watch ye, stand fast in the faith, quit you like men, be strong. Let all your things be done with charity" (I Corinthians 16:13-14).

Watch. What does a man need to watch for? He needs to watch for the Lord's coming, lest he be unprepared (Matthew 24:42-44). "Behold, I come as a thief. Blessed is he that watcheth" (Revelation 16:15). He needs to watch in all things (II Timothy 4:5) and not be gullible in anything, "proving what is acceptable unto the Lord" (Ephesians 5:10).

Stand fast in the faith. "Only let your conversation be as it becometh the gospel of Christ: that whether I come and see you, or else be absent, I may hear of your affairs, that ye stand fast in one spirit, with one mind striving together for the faith of the gospel"(Philippians 1:27). Men need to strive together, working in unity for the advancement of the faith of the gospel.

Paul strongly warned Timothy that other damaging thoughts and practices would accompany a departure from the faith. "Now the Spirit speaketh expressly, that in the latter times some shall depart from the faith, giving heed to seducing spirits, and doctrines of devils; speaking lies in hypocrisy; having their conscience seared with a hot iron; forbidding to marry, and commanding to abstain from meats, which God hath created to be received with thanksgiving of them which believe and know the truth"(I Timothy 4:1-3).

At the close of Paul's life, he was thankful for having not departed from the faith. "For I am now ready to be offered, and the time of my departure is at hand. I have fought a good fight, I have finished my course, I have kept the faith: Henceforth there is laid up for me a crown of righteousness, which the Lord, the righteous judge, shall give me at that day: and not to me only, but unto all them also that love his appearing"(II Timothy 4:6-8).

Jude also expressed a desire to see men contending for the faith. "Beloved, when I gave all diligence to write unto you of the common salvation, it was needful for me to write unto you, and exhort you that ye should earnestly contend for the faith which was once delivered unto the saints"(Jude 3).

Quit yourselves like men. Paul was not intending for men to give up or "call it quits"; rather he encouraged them to conduct themselves like men. In all situations, the man is to take the manly way out, never the coward's way. A man does not make his load lighter by heaping undue amounts of problems upon others. He carries his fair share of the load and seeks to help the less fortunate in the bearing of theirs.

Be strong. Being strong in the Lord is a desirable trait. Paul was not writing of bulging biceps but rather strength of character and strength of will in pushing one's self to the completion of a task. When a man is strong, he can provide the leadership that God desires him to offer to his family and associates.

Let all your things be done with charity. All things means all things. Giving to the poor, disciplining of children, witnessing to others of God's salvation plan, addressing the other driver who raced to the parking place first, dealing with a fellow employee who made the entire group look bad in evaluation—all things means all things. Done in charity simply means done in love. This attitude will bring a proper balance to the strength of a man—strength will be tempered in love.

The transition from boy to man involves more than the mere passage of time. In other cultures there is a definite initiatory rite that marks a boy's becoming a man. This rite of passage is missing in our culture and augments the ambiguity of the crossing of this momentous threshold.

With or without a rite, the passage is important. In Paul's day, the Jewish culture had a rite of passage. Even so, Paul realized that manhood did not necessarily accompany the rite. "When I was a child, I spake as a child, I understood as a child, I thought as a child: but when I became a man, I put away childish things"(I Corinthians 13:11).

A simple declaration does not make a man. A boy becomes a man by his personal development, not by someone's declaration. A male, be he a child or an adult, becomes a man by attaining to higher levels of character such as responsibility and integrity.

Someone once said, "We need not worry so much about what man descends from—it's what he descends to that shames the human race." Males can descend to beasthood, or they can ascend to manhood.

Think and Believe Like a Man

With the development and accessibility of the personal computer, a new vocabulary is developing. One phrase is "garbage in—garbage out." What is programmed into a computer is what comes out. Most billing errors that were attributed to "computer error" were actually programmer error, an error of the human being that fed the information to the computer to start with, not in the calculation of the computer.

The same principle applies to mankind. "Garbage in—garbage out." A man is what he thinks. The wise man of Proverbs realized this and wrote an admonition to this effect: "For as he thinketh in his heart, so is he"(Proverbs 23:7).

Because of this, man must use caution in his choice of "mental stimulants." Since what we think on determines what we become, there are some things that should never be a part of our thinking.

There are some mental stimulants that come our way over which we have no control. These negative stimulants may cause an unclean thought to enter our minds, but we should turn away from unclean thinking immediately! "We cannot stop the birds from flying over our heads, but we can stop them from building a nest in our hair."

Other "mental stimulants" come our way because of choices we make. We choose to avoid the very appearance of evil (I Thessalonians 5:22) so that we may be good and not evil. A man will avoid pornography, whether it be hard core, soft core, or just a little bit questionable. He will guard his thinking, for in so doing, he will guard his being.

David knew the danger of watching a wicked thing. "I will set no wicked thing before mine eyes: I hate the work of them that turn aside; it shall not cleave to me"(Psalm 101:3). This admonition includes books, magazines, television, video, peep shows, and any other medium that would be a negative mental stimulant.

Things that reach us in ways other than the eye-gate, that is through the rest of the five senses, also need to be screened as a means of guarding our thinking and being.

Paul wrote, "Finally, brethren, whatsoever things are true, whatsoever things are honest, whatsoever things are just, whatsoever things are pure, whatsoever things are lovely, whatsoever things are of good report; if there be any virtue, and if there be any praise, think on these things"(Philippians 4:8).

Isaac Watts, in *Horace Lyricae,* wrote a poem that expresses the value of the thinking and of the mind.

"Were I so tall to reach the pole,
   Or grasp the ocean with my span,
I must be measured by my soul:
   The mind's the standard of the man."

The very foundation of a male being a man is for him to fear God. The wise writer of Proverbs penned these words: "Let us hear the conclusion of the whole matter: Fear God, and keep his commandments: for this is the whole duty of man"(Ecclesiastes 12:13).

Fearing God and obeying God is the whole duty of man. There can be no fear of God without a corresponding obedience of God's commandments.

Edwin Louis Cole, in *Courage,* deals with an interesting perspective. "That which is visible is created by that which is invisible." For example, loving is invisible, but giving is visible. Honor is invisible, but obedience is visible. By the same pattern of thinking, fear of God is invisible, but obedience is the visible outgrowth of it. Therefore, the fear of God is the foundation of a man; in fact it is the whole duty of man.

Two similar verses express this same principle. "The fear of the LORD is the beginning of wisdom"(Psalm 111:10). "The fear of the LORD is the beginning of knowledge"(Proverbs 1:7).

It is a necessary characteristic of a man that he fear the Lord. This is the beginning of the road to successful manhood.

Consider Job. He was "perfect and upright, and one that feared God, and eschewed evil"(Job 1:1). Because he feared God and hated evil, God used the word *perfect* to describe him. His wealth did not earn him this description from Deity. The size or quality of his family did not draw the Almighty's eye of approval. Instead, it was his fear of the Lord and his hatred of evil that drew God's commendations to him.

These attributes will still draw God's attention today. He is still looking for men who fear Him and hate evil.

The strength of a man's actions in a particular matter is determined by the power and intensity of his convictions regarding the matter. Someone once said, "What a man accomplishes depends on what he believes."

Men generally do what they want to do. When a desire to do the right thing about everything is the driving force of a man, he will be be steered in the right direction.

Virtue is another necessary ingredient in the make-up of a man. Pathagoras said, "Wealth is a weak anchor, and glory cannot support a man; this is the law of God, that virtue only is firm, and cannot be shaken by a tempest."

Dress Like a Man

The dress of a man is more than just his clothes. The attire of a man includes such things as his clothes, his posture, his manners, his spirit, his desires, his attitude, his hygiene—anything that can be seen and/or displayed. This is quite a list, and each will be addressed, although briefly.

Clothes. There are certain things in the Bible that are labeled as an "abomination unto the LORD thy God." For a man to wear things that are a woman's is one such abomination (Deuteronomy 22:5). Men should never wear women's garments, whether the garments are outer wear or underwear. Men would do well to use caution in the style, colors, materials and size of even the clothes that are intended for a man. Too tight, too effeminate, too dainty, too immodest—all such clothing should be avoided. That men dress like men is God's desire and commandment.

Men should dress for the occasion, providing they can maintain modesty and moderation. If the occasion dictates clothing that is either immodest or immoderate, the occasion needs to be avoided.

Posture. A man carries himself with dignity, but not with pride. He bows in the presence of God, but never slouches and slumps. He will walk with a manly stride, not an effeminate, prissy, mincing step. He will not be heavy handed or limp wristed.

Manners. A man is a gentleman. His courtesy will stand out in the rabble of the "base fellows." A gentlemen is not a brute with only brawn, but he has an alert, sensitive brain. He will honor women, revere the elderly, and love children. A study of manners is encouraged for any male desiring to become a man.

A mannerly, peaceful man will make a powerful impact on those around him. George William Curtis said, "To have known one good old man—one man who, through the chances and mischances of a long life, has carried his heart in his hand, like a palm branch, waving all discords into peace—helps our faith in God, in ourselves and in each other, more than many sermons."

Two accounts in the Book of Acts give acknowledgment to courteous men. "And Julius courteously entreated Paul, and gave him liberty to go unto his friends to refresh himself"(Acts 27:3), and "In the same quarters were possessions of the chief man of the island, whose name was Publius; who received us, and lodged us three days courteously"(Acts 28:7).

Spirit. "He that is slow to anger is better than the mighty; and he that ruleth his spirit than he that taketh a city"(Proverbs 16:32). A man should seek always to control his own spirit. He will determine never to lose his temper. "A man is like steel; when he loses his temper, he loses his strength." This verse of Scripture and the adage both serve to accent the need to control our own spirit.

Desires. Jesus taught His disciples to desire the things of God first. "But seek ye first the kingdom of God, and his righteousness; and all these things shall be added unto you"(Matthew 6:33). David, the man after God's own heart, put it this way: "O God, thou art my God; early will I seek thee: my soul thirsteth for thee, my flesh longeth for thee in a dry and thirsty land, where no water is; To see thy power and thy glory, so as I have seen thee in the sanctuary"(Psalm 63:1-2).

Attitudes. One of the greatest attitudes a man can have is an attitude of gratitude. It is difficult for a man to be great without being grateful. Thanksgiving, worship, and praise for God are normal coming from the mouth of a man. Unthankful men are a sign of the last days and the coming of perilous times.

Hygiene. A man may have the nicest of clothes, but if they are not clean or he is not clean, he will still be lacking. It is understandable that at times a man will get dirty and sweaty—working on a car, mowing a lawn, being physically active in a sport or other endeavor. The problem is when he stays dirty. A shower, shave, and shampoo work wonders. Bad breath, body odor, and other hygiene problems can detract from a man's being his best.

Summary

A crowning achievement of a male is to be a God-fearing man. This is God's desire and design. By thinking, believing, and dressing like a man, this goal can be attained. With the fear of God as the foundation, and being built up as a holy temple of God, God's men can march forth victoriously, more than conquerors through Christ.

Test Your Knowledge

1. What is a crowning achievement for a male?
2. What are the five admonitions given by Paul in I Corinthians 16:13-14?
3. Does a rite of passage cause a boy to become a man?
4. How does the phrase "garbage in—garbage out" relate to a man?
5. What are mental stimulants? How do they affect what a person becomes?
6. What is the whole duty of man?
7. What are some of the things which make up a man's attire?
8. Is God concerned about the way a man dresses?
9. What man is better than he who takes a city?
10. It is difficult for a man to be great without being grateful. What is perhaps the greatest attitude a man can possess?

Apply Your Knowledge

After having read and studied the information given in this chapter, look to yourself and consider your habits, attire, and thoughts. Do you feel that you need some improvement? Why not ask for God's help in being a man. After all, that is His desire for you.

Expand Your Knowledge

To add to the material contained in this chapter, consider two books by Edwin Louis Cole: *Maximized Manhood, A Guide to Family Survival,* and *Courage, A Book for Champions*. These books contain information that will help in your striving for true manhood.

4. Spirituality and Christian Service

And if it seem evil unto you to serve the LORD, choose you this day whom ye will serve; whether the gods which your fathers served that were on the other side of the flood, or the gods of the Amorites, in whose land ye dwell: but as for me and my house, we will serve the LORD.

Joshua 24:15

Start With the Scriptures

Psalm 17:15
I Timothy 4:8-16; 6:10-12

II Timothy 3:12-17
I Peter 3:10

A certain bumper sticker has a very sad but often true description of many in society today. "Don't follow me—I'm lost." Perhaps this saying is displayed in jest, but the closer we examine these words in a broader context, the truer to life they become. It is needful that we have a clear understanding of goals worthy of our finest efforts.

Goal Setting

What are the objectives we wish to achieve? Are we obeying the commands of Jesus as He taught the people saying, "But seek ye first the kingdom of God"? It is needful that we as individuals and especially as heads of family units practice this in order to offer proper, effective leadership.

It should always be the expressed or implied desire of the Christian man that those given into his care would be true followers of Jesus Christ. It should be the desire of the Christian man that his family give themselves to godly principles. He need not lead dogmatically, but he should lead by the example of his own life. His leadership will be reflected in the value system that becomes the standard in his family unit.

A vocation is often chosen by a person simply because as a child he grew up surrounded by the activities that go along with the job. A person's ways of dealing with his problems are often an extension of his parents before him. If poor business practices are used, it is a good chance that this same faulty approach will be passed on. In view of these practical truths we observe in and about us, it becomes important that we start our spiritual journey in the proper manner.

It is needful that we have a clear view of what is most important in life. David wrote, "One thing have I desired of the LORD, that will I seek after; that I may dwell in the house of the LORD all the days of my life, to behold the beauty of the LORD, and to enquire in his temple" (Psalm 27:4).

We learn more from example than we do by mere spoken words. This is especially true within the home. It is time to ask ourselves probing questions. "What do I wish my children to become?" "What kind of woman do I want my wife to mature into?"

Christian men should set goals and directions and then apply themselves to achieve them.

We do not choose our calling of service in the body of Christ; rather we make ourselves available to the direction of the Holy Ghost by living a life dedicated and submissive to God. Neither can we as fathers choose or foster upon any member of our family a calling to a particular ministry. This is the sovereign choice of God and we should leave it to Him.

The Future Begins Now

A farmer cannot be a double minded person. It is essential to success that he have a steadfastness of purpose. He cannot be fickle in his purpose, for unsureness destroys any hope of success. He must begin early in the year to prepare the soil before the grass and weeds take control. Successful men realize that the harvest is affected by what is done in the months before the combines and harvesting machines enter the field. A farmer puts forth much effort and expense with the awareness that the future begins now; that which is hoped for and expected will only materialize if he begins today. "Behold, the husbandman waiteth for the precious fruit of the earth, and hath long patience for it, until he receive the early and latter rain" (James 5:7).

It is a human weakness to put off until tomorrow that which should be done today. If we are to reach our greatest potential in the Lord, we cannot wait and procrastinate for some more favorable time.

Life is made up of seasons, and we are challenged to do everything in the proper season. There is a time to till the soil, a time to plant, and then a time to reap the harvest. These cannot be rearranged without disrupting the outcome.

The future begins now and we cannot become careless or indifferent toward the opportunity that belongs to the Christian father. Solomon wrote, "They made me the keeper of the vineyards; but mine own vineyard have I not kept" (Song of Solomon 1:6). Harvest is determined today based upon how we apply ourselves in each given stage of life. We take hold of the task willingly, for in doing so we reap a great reward.

He Should Lead Spiritually

The demands placed upon the wage earner and the peer pressure to maintain a certain lifestyle has placed great stress upon the family unit. Often the father and sometimes the mother are absent for most of the waking hours of children. This adds great importance to the family time that is available.

We live in such a rushed and hurried age that family time is not an accident but the result of planning. Family time should be a pleasant time of interaction where the bonds of family are strengthened. It is during these times that discussion can be led into spiritually productive learning sessions. The spiritual man will use family time to good advantage even though it may be physically taxing. This need not be a time of lecture, but of games and learning with an objective to convey values that will give basis for future problem solving.

A definite ingredient that must accompany family time is love where each member of the family feels that he is wanted and appreciated. This time can and should be the adhesive that bonds the family into one strong unit, capable of meeting and overcoming the evil forces that war against the soul.

These family times should also include family prayer. Prayer time can be a marvelous adventure into the things of God. Prayer should not be approached as a drab duty to perform in order to avoid the harsh judgment of God, but a time of opportunity to talk to God in a very personal way.

The Christian man who aspires to properly guide his family must realize that help is needed in the challenges of life's complex questions. Thus he must be also a partaker of this practice of personal devotions. There are many helpful books on parenting that are available today, but above and beyond all these we need the special touch of God upon us to fulfill the task of being a real spiritual leader in the home. The man of God is encouraged to "pray without ceasing" (I Thessalonians 5:17). A consistent, prayerful lifestyle will afford personal strength and bring a greater sense of stability to others upon whom we have influence.

Jesus taught that "men ought always to pray, and not to faint" (Luke 18:1). One man has observed, "As my greatest business is for God, to serve Him, so my daily business is with God, to ask Him for strength to do it." If we continue in prayer we shall receive renewed strength from day to day to meet obstacles.

When we become parents, our children look to us. We need to have within ourselves the calm assurance of God's faithfulness, projecting to our children our confidence in the Master's watchful care. It was a strong force of faith that worked in Paul and Silas as they sang at midnight in the jail at Philippi. It was not the convenience of the moment or their physical well-being that prompted their song in the midnight hour. Rather it was their unwavering faith in God.

Faith caused the apostle Paul to proclaim, "Be of good cheer" (Acts 27:22) even though the storm yet raged and the winds were still buffeting. Paul's active expression of faith influenced every man on the ship.

Paul had a beloved disciple whom he referred to as his son in the gospel. This young man, Timothy, was called by God into the ministry. Timothy became the focus of Paul's attention in two letters, I and II Timothy, in which Paul, the aging apostle, desired to impart to this young man truths that would help him to take up the mantle of leadership and service.

Timothy was a young man and could become subject to certain fads and practices that could hinder his spirituality. Paul cautioned, "For bodily exercise profiteth little: but godliness is profitable unto all things, having promise of the life that now is, and of that which is to come" (I Timothy 4:8). It is apparent that certain benefits are derived from bodily exercise, but we must use caution and restraint lest the precious time given to us be used in a manner that will not profit in eternal rewards.

The Christian man must not be so entangled with the affairs of this life as to lose sight of the heavenly vision. Many things may not be so inherently evil as to immediately destroy, but they may have a burdening effect as Paul described when he wrote, "laying aside every weight."

The Christian man, in order to maintain his spiritual position before God, must heed the advice of Paul: "And every man that striveth for the mastery is temperate in all things" (I Corinthians 9:25). He can become so involved in pleasurable activities until they become a detriment to his walk with God.

Timothy was advised, "Take heed to thyself" (I Timothy 4:16). This may seem strange in the face of this man's favorable background and his early childhood. An inherent human weakness is that we often examine others but fail to consider our life in the light of what the Lord expects of us. It is essential to our spiritual life that we hear the preaching of God's Word and allow it to become a mirror in which we see ourselves. God has deemed that we may be saved by the ministry of the preached Word.

It is an unwise thing to compare ourselves with others, to seek to find justification for our conduct by the way others live. We are challenged to strive to measure up to the stature of Christ.

In Psalm 119:9 a question is asked and then an answer is given. "Wherewithal shall a young man cleanse his way? by taking heed thereto according to thy word." God in His sovereign wisdom has designed a plan whereby we may both see ourselves and also understand how to remedy situations that may exist. Since anointed preaching is the most powerful force known for correcting the mistakes and misconceptions of mankind, it must always hold a prominent place in the life of the Christian.

The Christian must not be deceived as some were when they thought that gain was godliness (I Timothy 6:6). The lure of materialism has often crowded out the chance for the spiritual man to prosper. This enticement is so deceptive that we may not recognize its subtle approach to our lives. The desire for riches may be as the proverbial pot of gold at the end of the rainbow, a force that leads us on so many fruitless journeys until our days are used up, all our tomorrows become yesterdays, and we still have not arrived at the place of contentment. Paul pointed out to Timothy that "godliness with contentment is great gain" (I Timothy 6:6). Things do not satisfy by themselves, but Jesus abiding as Lord of our lives brings real satisfaction.

Jesus said, "Lay not up for yourselves treasures upon earth, where moth and rust doth corrupt, and where thieves break through and steal" (Matthew 6:19). Then in a later verse He gave the reason why this is so dangerous: "For where your treasure is, there will your heart be also" (Matthew 6:21).

Paul's concern for Timothy's spiritual welfare was based upon the bedrock of truth that no man can serve two masters. We cannot give undivided loyalty and service to two opposing forces that war in the spiritual realm.

The teachings of Jesus do not say that a Christian will have a life of want and need, but that he can expect many blessings both material and spiritual.

The Christian man develops the understanding that all things are of God. He is the giver of every good and perfect gift and as such He expects us to honor Him with the increase of our substance. The individual who honors God with tithes and offerings is acknowledging the source of supply. When tithes and offerings are given in a proper attitude, it is a beautiful act of worship. This should reduce the human inclination to heap together treasure without regard to honoring the great giver of all things.

He Should Lead to Church

In a world plagued by high crime rates and decaying morals that erode and undermine the foundations of society, there is a source of hope. Consistent church attendance will provide a strong counterbalance to the forces that are faced in daily living. The truly spiritual person finds church attendance a joy. He does not regard it as simply a duty, but a wonderful privilege. The psalmist wrote, "I was glad when they said unto me, Let us go into the house of the LORD" (Psalm 122:1).

The person who strives for mastery in spiritual matters is willing to expend the energy and take ample time to be loyal to all the activities of the local church. The person who has trouble with consistent church attendance is often one who derives no joy from the experience, who simply goes out of duty, who neither sees the glory nor appreciates the great things that take place in the assembly of the faithful. The person striving for spiritual excellence will make every effort to be in the house of God.

Another factor in the spiritual person's life is the act of worship. Jesus spoke of a time when "true worshippers shall worship the Father in spirit and in truth: for the Father seeketh such to worship him" (John 4:23). Worship must consist of more than mere rituals that promote formality in worship. Worship that lifts the soul and refreshes the individual will cause one to rise upon wings of joy and soar above the difficulties that presently surround him. Worship that is heartfelt is a means by which God restores and renews the inward man.

The act of our leading in worship contributes a positive influence upon those around us. It is in these seasons of worship that lasting impressions are imprinted upon the children entrusted to our care. What fond memories fill many adults today as they recall childhood days of attendance in the house of God with parents who practiced genuine worship. The Christian man must be willing and able to lead in this very important function of successful Christian living.

Within the body of true believers in the local assembly lies a strength in the bonds of brotherhood. This strength helps the weak regain their spiritual vigor and become overcomers. The strength of Christian fellowship with believers is but another means God has in His great plan to bring many sons into glory.

He Should Lead to Service

Our Lord in His marvelous concern for the church has given it a five-fold ministry to bring to perfection those who are obedient to the gospel. Paul pointed out to the Ephesians that God "gave some, apostles; and some, prophets; and some, evangelists; and some, pastors and teachers" (Ephesians 4:11). Our Lord prepared the needed ministries to perfect a church and equip it to meet the needs of all mankind.

God has given pastors to the church who will influence our lives for good, men who have a "shepherd's heart." A good shepherd closely identifies with his sheep. He is not trying to tend sheep by proxy, but he lives among them, sharing their joys as well as their times of sadness. The spiritually-minded man is conscious of the great pastoral blessing God placed in the body of Christ and he therefore forges a strong bond of love and respect, realizing that the pastor has been set over him as a watchman on the wall. The parent that wishes to help secure the future of his children will support the pastor in prayer, being readily available to assist in any task that is assigned. The truly enlightened person does not gripe, complain, or speak harshly of that individual whom God has set as a watchman over that flock.

It is needful that spiritual men and women give their time and talents toward reaching the lost and expanding the influence of the local church. Many programs are utilized by various churches in seeking to fulfill the command of our Lord to go into all the world and preach the gospel to every person. If a man has the correct relationship with Christ, he will want to be involved. It is a joy to feel that we have had a part in someone finding salvation. The wisdom of God is so complete that we are awed by the discovery that while we help others we often help ourselves.

Parents that reap the greatest rewards do so by setting proper examples in all areas of Christian stewardship. Example conveys truth to children. Most all local assemblies have educational programs, choirs, and youth services. We should set the direction for those we wish to see prosper in spiritual matters. The spiritually-minded parent will cooperate in and be in attendance for these functions faithfully. The truth of the proverb, "Train up a child in the way he should go" (Proverbs 22:6), becomes a reality when it is practiced by the parent and spiritual leader of the home. A Christian should recognize that it is a joyful opportunity to participate in the programs of the church and not merely a sacrificial duty. If we will do God's will with our whole heart, many great blessings will be ours to experience.

To seek a life of spirituality and to be joyously involved in the work of God in a local assembly are keys to maturity and happiness. It is a joy to watch the development and growth of those whom God has entrusted to our care. It provides a basis for fulfillment and inward satisfaction. The apostle John wrote, "I have no greater joy than to hear that my children walk in truth" (III John 4). Walking in truth, growing into maturity, and assuming the role to which God has called us is a goal worthy of our finest abilities and deepest commitment. It simply will be seen at the end of the race that those who applied themselves are winners.

Test Your Knowledge

1. ____ _____ should always be our guide in setting spiritual goals.
2. Children often choose a vocation because of _____ _____.
3. When should preparations be made for a spiritual harvest?
4. The husbandman must be first a partaker of what?
5. The family leader must give _____ and _____ to family devotions.
6. Jesus taught that men ought always to pray and not to _____.

7. A strong faith in God gives _____ to a Christian's walk.

8. In I Timothy 4:16 Paul advised Timothy to take heed unto whom?

9. The person who strives for the mastery is _____ in all things.

10. To enjoy a full reward one must do what?

Expand Your Knowledge

Without making comments observe those of your acquaintance that have enjoyed success in walking with God. Notice some families that have two or more generations that serve God faithfully and consider their strengths.

Next, take a time of prayer and fasting where you look inward and examine your daily and weekly activities. Note how Timothy was a third generation person of a household whose faith had impressed the apostle Paul. Read both I Timothy and II Timothy.

Apply Your Knowledge

Every child of God must walk circumspectly or with deliberate intent and purpose. After reading this lesson and considering it in prayer, make some commitments to be more effective in personal relationships. Privately list areas you wish to improve in, not speaking of this openly, but simply set some personal goals.

If you are a parent, apply the Bible principles of this lesson and watch the results as they begin to materialize and be reproduced in your home.

Seek to present a positive approach to all the duties of Christian discipleship. Consciously remind yourself often that to be "Christlike" is our duty and our privilege as Spirit-filled believers.

5 Remaking Broken Vessels

And the vessel that he made of clay was marred in the hand of the potter: so he made it again another vessel, as seemed good to the potter to make it.
Jeremiah 18:4

Start With the Scriptures

Joshua 7:10-12   II Samuel 12:13, 19-25; 24:10

Failure need not be final. In fact, the Bible has a great deal to say to those who have sinned and fallen short. While not a single blessing is promised for failure, there are encouraging statements from Genesis to Revelation for the one who truly repents and forsakes his sin.

Let there be no mistake about it; sinning is deadly. Despite the modern trend to discount the consequences of spiritual failure, God takes the matter very seriously indeed. Habakkuk declared of the

Lord, "Thou art of purer eyes than to behold evil, and canst not look on iniquity" (Habakkuk 1:13). "Righteousness," Proverbs 14:34 states, "exalteth a nation: but sin is a reproach to any people." Sin, therefore, is a rebellion against one's own interests, and worse still, an offense towards the Almighty.

There would be nothing left but dismal defeat for every transgressor were it not for the Christian message. But Jesus came! He came to reveal the love and mercy of the Father. Without Christ the world would have been left without an adequate witness. "No man hath seen God at any time; the only begotten Son, which is in the bosom of the Father, he hath declared him" (John 1:18).

The multiple transgressions of men require—yes, demand—that a just God punish sin to the full extent. To do less would condone what the Scriptures condemn. It would serve to make a mockery of any sense of right and wrong. It would prove the Lord both partial and prejudiced.

How thankful we should be for the provision that was made at Calvary. While the sacrifice of Christ was made once for all (Hebrews 10:12), the amazing fact remains that individuals may continually find mercy through the cross. The blood of Christ provides a fountain of forgiveness which never runs dry. A man, coming in repentance time and time again, will find a Savior ready and able to pardon his transgressions.

You Can Come Back

The Pharisees and scribes, so often agitated by Jesus Christ, were once again murmuring at His behavior. This time they complained, "This man receiveth sinners, and eateth with them" (Luke 15:2). To the Pharisees and scribes it seemed scandalous that the Lord would cordially, even affectionately, welcome the tax collectors and other transgressors of the law. How could He associate with those outcasts from society and still maintain any sense of respectability?

This bitter attack from His enemies failed to deter the Lord. Instead Jesus used their agitation to show how it contrasted with God's attitude toward the sinner. In three beautiful parables (the lost sheep, Luke 15:3-7; the lost coin, Luke 15:8-10; and the lost son, 15:11-32), our Lord drew a glorious picture of the Father's love for the outcast.

Possibly the most famous and most treasured of all Christ's parables deals with a son who demanded and received his inheritance. "Father," this younger of two sons boldly requested, "give me the portion of goods that falleth to me" (Luke 15:12).

The waywardness of this younger son was total. He seemed to have had no concern for anything but his own pleasure. He was sensual and selfish. And like so many other prodigals, he wasted every penny he received from his father.

The common people who heard Jesus must have been fascinated by the brief description of the prodigal's disaster. "And when he had spent all, there arose a mighty famine in that land; and he began to be in want" (Luke 15:14). The once proud son was lowered to the point where he fed the swine, "and no man gave unto him" (Luke 15:16). It was a colossal fall for one who had been so independent.

The story, however, did not end there, for Jesus went on to say that the son "came to himself" (Luke 15:17). The truth is that every practicing sinner is somewhat deranged, especially if he has once known the power of the Holy Ghost. Nothing seems more ridiculous than to think that worldly pleasure could really replace heavenly joy. We are truly fools when we allow Satan to lead us toward the "pig pen."

The amazing thing was that the prodigal son did

come to himself. Sin hardens the heart, and the distance back home from the "far country" might seem insurmountable. But the son's situation was simply awful, and without food or friends, he had time to reflect on his father's provisions. The prodigal questioned himself, "How many hired servants of my father's have bread enough and to spare, and I perish with hunger!" (Luke 15:17).

Two things encouraged the wayward young man. First, he was still a son, though he no longer felt worthy of any family benefits. Second, he felt assured that the father would at least listen to his plea. These two factors—family relationship and fatherly concern—made a terrific difference.

The prodigal "arose" (something that every sinner must do if he is to escape destruction). No one else could have done that for him. For the prodigal it was more than just talk; it became a walk.

The story says, "But when he was yet a great way off, his father saw him, and had compassion, and ran, and fell on his neck, and kissed him" (Luke 15:20). The Greek verb translated "to have compassion" means "to be moved inwardly" or "to yearn for a sufferer." It is the same word that is used of Christ in Matthew 9:36 and 14:14. A father's heart was touched by the sight of his son's ruin.

The father not only saw but he understood. If there had ever been any thought of the injustice done to himself, the parent immediately forgot it. The pain of separation was displaced by the joy of reunion. One thing and only one thing mattered. "This my son was dead, and is alive again; he was lost, and is found" (Luke 15:24).

Nothing was too good for the one who was restored. We can imagine the servants scurrying to find the best robe, a fine ring, and suitable shoes for the prodigal. The stall-fed calf had to be butchered and preparations made for a banquet. Yet nothing speaks as loudly of God's love as those first impulsive actions of the father as he "ran and embraced him and kissed him—fervently" (Luke 15:20, *The Amplified Bible*).

Sad to say, while the younger son was restored, we are uncertain about his brother. The elder son had lost something far more valuable than a portion of the inheritance. What he had lost was his sense of mercy. Not only was he unforgiving towards his brother, he was offended at his father. Like the scribes and Pharisees, the offended one could see no reason to rejoice over the homecoming of a wretched sinner.

You Haven't Gone Too Far

Backsliding always entails a journey away from God. Step by step men depart from the principles of the Bible. It is not so much that the Lord leaves us; rather the scriptural evidence points to the fact that we leave Him. According to Genesis 4:16, "Cain went out from the presence of the LORD," and Judas, on the night he betrayed Jesus, "having received the sop went immediately out: and it was night" (John 13:30).

Neither is it only the willfully wicked who find themselves at a distance from the Lord. "Peter followed him afar off" (Matthew 26:58), and many a well-intentioned man has discovered that his relationship with God has become cold and estranged.

The sensitive individual feels undone. Like Peter, he may find that he betrayed a sacred trust. By words or by actions he denied his Master. A man may sharply reproach himself for his own unfaithfulness. Following Peter's terrible downfall, Matthew 26:75 says of that apostle, "He went out, and wept bitterly."

It is here that a person must make a vital decision.

Will he walk further on in the direction of worldliness and sin, or will he turn around and head back home? The way back to God may appear to be all uphill, but heaven cheers every repentant sinner on. (See Luke 15:7, 10.)

The individual has not gone too far from God as long as he is willing to repent. Repentance is a change of mind or purpose. The obligation cannot be placed upon the Lord; it rests upon the individual's shoulders. God does not need to change; the individual needs to change. Just like His truth and like His righteousness, God's mercy endures forever.

A man, by continuously hardening himself against the mercy of God, may eventually destroy his own faith. (See Ephesians 4:30; I Timothy 1:19.) This is never the divine purpose, however. According to II Peter 3:9, the Lord "is longsuffering to us-ward, not willing that any should perish, but that all should come to repentance."

The Lord simply does not throw His children out the front door when they fail. They may rebel and leave in a huff on their own, but He keeps the "porch light burning."

You Can Rebuild

Failure has a way of humbling us, of breaking us, and of remaking us. The fellow who seldom fails seldom accomplishes much either. To look at life honestly, to admit one's mistakes and then to push on is what really counts. Failure, like sorrow, can be a great teacher.

During the Second World War a group of American soldiers were pinned down by enemy fire on a beach in Normandy. The bullets from German weapons were withering, and those G.I.'s who had not been killed had found cover. A sergeant huddled behind a burnt-out tank saw how serious a situation the Americans were in. Waving his buddies on, the sergeant led an attack that eventually drove the enemy back.

Yes, failure is bitter, and it is frustrating. The sky seems heavy with clouds when we fail, and we are prone to imagine that others have life far easier. If we are not careful, we can become defensive and critical. We often struggle as much with our emotions as with our circumstances.

Beyond the stinging sensation of defeat, however, there is hope. Failure need not be final. In fact, the crushing of our wills through disappointment may be the very thing that is needful. The Lord still uses broken things to manifest His glory.

In chapter eighteen of the Book of Jeremiah the prophet was instructed by the Lord to go to the potter's house. The clay in the workman's hands was being molded on the wheels, but the vessel was marred in the hands of the potter. As Jeremiah watched, he saw the same clay made over into another vessel.

The whole account was a graphic illustration of God's dealings with Israel. Though brought out from the land of Egypt, the nation had failed to become the vessel of honor the Lord had intended. Still His people were not discarded as useless. Rather the Potter did His best with what He had and made something new.

We, too, may not be all that God has intended. Like the marred vessel which Jeremiah saw, there may be something in our nature which stubbornly resists the will of the Potter—a quantity of grit or sand, a bit of unyielding clay. It is not up to us to tell the Master Craftsman what we should be. Paul the apostle was first broken on the road to Damascus; then the Lord informed Ananias, "He is a chosen vessel unto me" (Acts 9:15). Paul himself declared, "Shall the thing formed say to him that formed it, Why hast thou made me thus? Hath not the potter power over the clay, of the same lump to make one vessel unto honour, and another unto dishonour?" (Romans 9:20-21).

Fred H. Wight made this interesting observation regarding a Palestinian potter. "He makes this wheel spin around, as he shapes the clay with his hands into a cone-shaped figure. Then he uses his thumb to make a hole in the top of the whirling clay, and keeps opening it until he can put his left hand inside of it" (Wight, F. H., *Manners and Customs of Bible Lands,* Moody Press, page 204).

Painstakingly the Lord will work in a man's heart and lead him into righteousness. This is not divine coercion. Rather it is divine direction. "For it is God which worketh in you both to will and to do of his good pleasure" (Philippians 2:13).

There are no higher goals than those which lie before a Christian. The Bible never promises an easy ascent, but it does show us that through faith and consistent living the spiritual climb can be successful. Perhaps it is here that many fail, because they have come to believe in instant success and easy solutions. The courage to hold on in tough situations, to forbear under pressure, is essential. The spiritual life has no credit cards; we have to pay the price as we go along.

As a man, one must build the kind of Christ-centered life that is truly satisfying. If he has seriously failed, then he needs to start to rebuild. He must clear away the debris of past disappointments and failures, dig deep, and commit himself afresh to God. (See Matthew 7:24.) A man should live according to the principles of the New Testament and not according to his feelings or changing circumstances.

The rewards for rebuilding one's broken life are

astonishing. Areas of obvious weakness can eventually become areas of superior strength. Amazingly one will discover that God Himself is corroborating his efforts to reconstruct what the devil has torn down.

Do Something Now

If one wanders away from God he needs no other call to action than a sense of his own impending danger. A sailor in a sinking ship will act in desperate haste to save his own life and the lives of others. A father who wakes up to see his home on fire becomes a living dynamo of action.

When it comes to salvation, however, many in the face of disaster never move a muscle. They are like the twenty passengers in a railway car who disbelieved their conductor's warning of the approaching Johnstown flood. Those people perished, as did thousands of others, in a great destructive torrent.

Sometimes we want to wait. We want to contemplate. We want to postpone a decision. We are like Felix who, while trembling with conviction, told Paul the apostle, "Go thy way for this time; when I have a convenient season, I will call for thee" (Acts 24:25).

When a Christian sins he needs to turn quickly to God in repentance. No matter could be more urgent; none deserves more attention.

While men often treat sin as tolerable weakness, the Lord regards it as an accursed thing to be totally extinguished. After Israel's defeat at Ai, Joshua fell on his face in desperate prayer. The prayer was sincere, but God wanted something far more than words. "And the LORD said unto Joshua, Get thee up; wherefore liest thou thus upon thy face? Israel hath sinned. . . . neither will I be with you any more, except ye destroy the accursed from among you"

(Joshua 7:10-12). Either Joshua would remove sin from the nation or sin would remove him from the presence of the Almighty.

You Can Be Restored

Repentance will bring us back into harmony and fellowship with God. There will be that sense of well-being that only the Holy Ghost can bring. Why should we stand outside the Father's house, like an exile, when He has killed the fatted calf in our behalf?

Despite the accusations of Satan and perhaps those of an elder brother, God waits to seat us at His banqueting table. Our place has been vacated too long. See how He provides for our needs! David said, "My cup runneth over" (Psalm 23:5).

What a tribute it is to God's love that He will completely forgive the backslider. Far from taking the matter lightly or indifferently, the one who has been restored should be forever thankful. None other than God Himself could have been so gracious. In the words of David, "He restoreth my soul" (Psalm 23:3).

The Lord wishes to take our lives and shape them into vessels of blessing. If we are marred through our own disobedience, there is still hope. God will certainly continue to deal with us. As long as the clay remains soft and pliable in the hands of the potter it can be made over. If we will allow our Lord to mold us through His superior workmanship, the Lord will make us into something remarkably worthwhile.

Test Your Knowledge

1. Why must God judge sin?
2. How did the scribes and Pharisees react to Jesus when He befriended sinners?
3. What did Jesus teach in the parable of the prodigal son regarding a backslider's situation in "the far country"?
4. State two things which encouraged the prodigal to return home.
5. Describe the father's response to the son who had caused him shame.
6. What was the elder son's response?
7. What did Jeremiah see happen at the potter's house?
8. Why was the vessel marred in the hands of the potter?
9. Is a mental decision to repent sufficient?
10. What are some of the difficulties in getting back to God once a person has failed?

Apply Your Knowledge

Mercy is one of the outstanding attributes of God. We who have been saved are expected to convey love towards others.

We should ask ourselves, "How do I react towards those who have fallen deeply into sin but are struggling to recover themselves?" Does our attitude reflect that of the scribes and Pharisees?

Expand Your Knowledge

List some of the characters in the Bible whose lives showed that God's hand was upon them and who yielded readily to the divine touch. List others who were "broken vessels" but who were made into something new.

The Responsibility of Fatherhood 6

But if any provide not for his own, and specially for those of his own house, he hath denied the faith, and is worse than an infidel.

I Timothy 5:8

Start With the Scriptures

Deuteronomy 6:7
I Samuel 1
Psalm 127:3-5
Proverbs 13:24

Luke 2
I Corinthians 16:13-14
Ephesians 5:25; 6:1-4
Colossians 3:18-21

God created man with the ability to procreate. This ability, though, does not guarantee that the man will fulfill the responsibilities of fatherhood. Someone once said, "Any man can be a father, but it takes someone special to be a dad." This expression may appear sentimentally simplistic, but is true nonetheless.

In the days of barn dances, the host of the event would hire a fiddler to provide music for the square dancing. Since the host had the responsibility of pay-ing the fiddler, he also had the privilege of calling for the tunes that he wanted played. This practice gave birth to the expression, "He who pays the fiddler calls the tunes."

This truth can be stated in another way: "For every privilege, there is a corresponding responsibility." As long as an individual continues to act in a responsible fashion, he continues to enjoy the privileges. This is true in all walks of life, and in each successive age of life.

A true father is one who not only "calls the tunes" but who also "pays the fiddler." He enters into fatherhood only after making a commitment to the responsibility of fatherhood.

Provider

A man's commitment to the responsibilities of fatherhood is a noble one. Any man who does less is actually despicable in the eyes of God.

The Scriptures do not attempt to soften the picture of God's displeasure at those who ignore their responsibilities. Rather, it presents an accurate account of God's attitude; the man who does not live up to the responsibilities of fatherhood has denied the faith and is worse than an infidel. These are strong words, but yet they are the authentic expression of God's viewpoint in this matter. "But if any provide not for his own, and specially for those of his own house, he hath denied the faith, and is worse than an infidel" (I Timothy 5:8).

Love the Mother

One of the most important responsibilities of a father is to love his wife. There is a plaque that offers this nugget of wisdom: "The greatest gift a father can give a child is to love its mother." It is in the atmosphere of father loving mother that a child can feel most secure and loved.

Paul's instructions, "Husbands, love your wives" (Ephesians 5:25), lays down a foundational requirement for a man living up to the responsibility of fatherhood. This foremost criterion, when met, establishes an element of reason for the man's choosing to be burdened with responsibility rather than running from its seeming shackles. It is a giving up of selfish, self-centered attitudes and actions by the man (and the woman) and accepting the responsibility that comes with the union of man and woman.

Children—Heritage of the Lord

It is a natural feeling for a husband and wife to desire a child. This desire should be more than just a desire for something to pet, pamper, and rock. (A pet puppy could fulfill this.) The parents should look beyond the cooing and cuddling, and see the long term responsibilities involved.

Children are not to be considered "burdens" just because they are accompanied by responsibilities of mammoth proportions. God considers them as His heritage and reward. "Lo, children are an heritage of the LORD: and the fruit of the womb is his reward. As arrows are in the hand of a mighty man; so are children of the youth. Happy is the man that hath his quiver full of them" (Psalm 127:3-5).

It is an honorable longing when a God-fearing couple desires a child. When that desire is coupled with a desire to raise the child in the nurture and admonition of the Lord, God's richest blessings can be enjoyed.

The first chapter of I Samuel presents a story full of pathos and the power of prayer. Hannah, wife of Elkanah, was unable to bear children. She was provoked sorely by others because of her barren condition, but Elkanah loved her and showered a worthy portion of goods upon her. The things, however, did not satisfy Hannah. She wanted a son.

She went to Shiloh and prayed for a "man child." As she prayed, she said, "O LORD of hosts, if thou wilt indeed look on the affliction of thine handmaid, and remember me, and not forget thine handmaid, but wilt give unto thine handmaid a man child, then I will give him unto the LORD all the days of his life, and there shall no razor come upon his head" (I Samuel 1:11).

Eli the priest noticed her manner of praying and thought that she was drunken. After being assured that she was earnestly petitioning God, Eli sent her out in peace, with the promise that God would grant her petition. God kept His part of the bargain, and so did Hannah.

Fatherhood

True fatherhood involves more than just husband and wife. A third ingredient needs be added—that of a child. It is this addition to the family unit that brings about the awesome responsibility of fatherhood, yet the responsibility should be faced squarely before the baby arrives. Some things need to be addressed and settled before the birth.

Not only must layette and crib be acquired, but the husband and wife need to feel secure in each other and in God. As they establish proper priorities in the home and create a loving, spiritual atmosphere, the addition of more responsibility will not be "a straw that breaks the camel's back." Dad will have already assumed the responsibility of providing loving leadership for the family of two. The arrival of the third member of the family will not upset the structure of authority but rather enhance it.

It has been said that the way to find out how a young man will treat his bride-to-be is to watch how he treats his mother. If this is true, the way a boy learns how to treat his mother is by watching how his dad treats her. This repetitive cycle augments the importance of a man assuming fatherhood responsibility before ever becoming a father.

Sharing Responsibility

There is a big difference between sharing and avoiding the responsibilities of parenting. A wise father will not pass the responsibility on to the shoulders of the mother.

In avoiding responsibilities the man would be saying,"Dear, you are responsible for bathing, clothing, feeding, and training this child. Let me know when he is old enough and mature enough for me to enjoy; then I'll enter the picture again." Sharing the responsibilities would be when the husband and wife work together to clothe, feed, bathe, and train the child, working in harmony as the husband leads.

The second chapter of Luke records the birth of Jesus Christ. Although Joseph was not the actual father, he assumed the responsibility of fatherhood. He did this willingly, with little or no concern for the negative effects it would have on him and his reputation. He shared the parental responsibilities, being willing to assume the leadership role.

In verses four and five, Joseph traveled with Mary to Bethlehem to be taxed. In verses six and seven Joseph was with Mary when Jesus was born. In verse sixteen Joseph was with Mary when they received the shepherds. In verse twenty-two Mary and Joseph brought Jesus to the Temple for His circumcision. In verse twenty-four they brought an offering. In verse forty-one Mary and Joseph went to the Temple regularly. In verse forty-five they sought for Jesus, and in verse forty-six they found Him. Mary and Joseph constantly shared the responsibilities of the Christ child. This is an excellent pattern for present day dads to follow.

One of the most precious times of commitment for a family or an individual is that of a baby dedication. Each pastor probably follows a similar pattern during this service.

It is at this time that the parents place the baby into the arms of the pastor, who is standing in the Lord's stead. The parents are showing their desire and their intention to surrender their child to the Lord—to His saving power, keeping power, healing power, and His guiding power. The pastor will generally pray a dedication prayer, not as a rite of salvation but instead as a sincere petition to God for assistance in raising the child. Often the pastor anoints both the father and the mother and prays for God to help them and give them wisdom and grace for the difficult yet rewarding task of raising the child.

Following this prayer, the pastor will sometimes place the child back into the hands of the father, symbolizing the proper role of spiritual leadership possessed by him. With this ceremony of commitment comes a fresh glimpse of the awesome responsibility of fatherhood.

Provoke Not

Paul, in writing to the Ephesians, dealt with the responsibilities of children to parents and that of the fathers to children. "Children, obey your parents in the Lord: for this is right. Honour thy father and mother; (which is the first commandment with promise;) That it may be well with thee, and thou mayest live long on the earth. And, ye fathers, provoke not your children to wrath: but bring them up in the nurture and admonition of the Lord" (Ephesians 6:1-4).

It is the responsibility of the father to correct and

discipline his child, but it should always be administered in love. "He that spareth his rod hateth his son: but he that loveth him chasteneth him betimes" (Proverbs 13:24).

When a child is provoked, annoyed, or vexed by a father, a common respect is sometimes damaged. This respect is a fragile thing and needs to be nurtured.

Teasing one another within a family circle can be done in fun. Sometimes, though, it goes too far. If a father teases a child in an unmerciful fashion, heedless of the effect, the child may be provoked and seek to respond in an angry or disrespectful manner. At this point, the father needs to use wisdom and caution in correcting the resulting actions since he has actually provoked the child to that point.

Parents, and fathers in particular, would do well to consider their children and "provoke unto love and to good works" (Hebrews 10:24). Since the influence of a father over a child is great, whether for good or evil, wisdom urges that his influence be for good.

Paul wrote a similar passage to the Colossians in which he addressed several different relationships. "Wives, submit yourselves unto your own husbands, as it is fit in the Lord. Husbands, love your wives, and be not bitter against them. Children, obey your parents in all things: for this is well pleasing unto the Lord. Fathers, provoke not your children to anger, lest they be discouraged" (Colossians 3:18-21).

As Paul dealt with the father and child relationship, he instructed fathers to provoke not a child, lest the child become discouraged. Discouragement is a difficult emotion to overcome. A child especially has difficulty because of a shortage of positive experiences in overcoming difficulties. Having no ready arsenal with which to fight discouragement places a child at a disadvantage. A wise father will strive to be an encourager, one who builds up, rather than a discourager, or one who tears down.

A Teacher

In chapter five of Deuteronomy, we are reminded that God gave the Ten Commandments to Moses. Moses passed them on to the people of Israel with these instructions: "Thou shalt teach them diligently unto thy children, and shalt talk of them when thou sittest in thine house, and when thou walkest by the way, and when thou liest down, and when thou risest up" (Deuteronomy 6:7).

It is imperative that a father teach his children the ways of God. It should not be relegated to the mother only. A father should realize the importance of passing on to his children a Christian heritage, teaching them by both word and deed, explaining the Word of God and exampling the Word of God.

Joshua realized the importance of keeping the nation's spiritual heritage for later generations. After the people of Israel passed over the Jordan River, Joshua had a man from each tribe to take a stone out of the midst of the river and place it on the river's bank. Joshua said, "That this may be a sign among you, that when your children ask their fathers in time to come, saying, What mean ye by these stones? Then ye shall answer them, That the waters of Jordan were cut off before the ark of the covenant of the LORD; when it passed over Jordan, the waters of Jordan were cut off: and these stones shall be for a memorial unto the children of Israel for ever" (Joshua 4:6-7).

One of the major responsibilities of fatherhood is to pass on to each succeeding generation the knowledge and understanding of God and His love for His people.

Petitioning the Master

In chapter four of his Gospel, John recorded an incident that depicts a concerned and caring father. This father, a nobleman whose son was sick, came to Jesus and pleaded with Him to come to Capernaum and heal his son who was at the point of death. In faith, the nobleman petitioned the master saying, "Sir, come down ere my child die." Jesus, being moved perhaps by the father's faith and persistence, answered, "Go thy way; thy son liveth." The nobleman believed the words of Jesus and went back home. His servants met him with the victorious report that his son was alive.

This miracle took place because a father was moved out of passiveness and into prayerfulness.

Fathers today will be amazed at the power of prayer. Petitioning Jesus on behalf of our children makes a difference. Intercession for our children's sake is another major responsibility of fatherhood.

Summary

Malachi wrote of a turning "the heart of the fathers to the children, and the heart of the children to their fathers" (Malachi 4:6). God, in His wisdom and power, is able to accomplish a bond between a father and his children if the father follows and trusts Him.

Fathers can accept the challenge Paul wrote to the Corinthians: "Watch ye, stand fast in the faith, quit you like men, be strong. Let all your things be done with charity" (I Corinthians 16:13-14). In so doing, they accept and fulfill the responsibility of fatherhood.

Test Your Knowledge

True or False

_____ 1. A man should enter fatherhood only after making a commitment to the responsibility of fatherhood.

_____ 2. God does not condemn a man for being slack in his responsibilities of being a father.

_____ 3. One of the most important responsibilities of fatherhood is to love the child's mother.

_____ 4. Children are a curse of the Lord.

_____ 5. The best time to face the responsibility of fatherhood is while the baby is in kindergarten.

_____ 6. A father should shoulder little responsibility for the religious training of his child.

_____ 7. Discipline should always be administered in love.

_____ 8. Teasing is a dangerous thing.

_____ 9. "Do as I say, not as I do," is not a fitting motto for a father raising a child.

_____ 10. Jesus responds to praying parents.

Apply Your Knowledge

After having read and studied this chapter, perhaps you have come to understand your strong and weak points as a parent. Consider your ways, noting I Corinthians 16:13-14. This challenge needs to be accepted and acted upon. Look for ways to improve as a father. Strive in the coming days to seek for God's divine wisdom in becoming a better father of God's precious heritage.

Expand Your Knowledge

For further reading and study, consider the book, *Maximized Manhood,* by Edwin Louis Cole. It will serve to add emphasis to this important subject.

Teaching Principles and Standards to Children

7

Train up a child in the way he should go: and when he is old, he will not depart from it.

Proverbs 22:6

Start With the Scriptures

Deuteronomy 5, 6, 7
Joshua 4:1-24; 24:15
Hebrews 11:23-26

The responsibility of training a child is one of the most awesome challenges a man will face in his lifetime. The weight of that responsibility is inescapable.

Every Christian father should be concerned about his ability to establish his faith in the hearts of his children. Many parents eagerly purchase the latest books by the best authors concerning proper child rearing in hope that the book may have some "secret" that has been missed before. While many books do indeed offer advice that is helpful, there are no secrets, of course—only old truths restated in modern language.

This lesson seeks to rediscover some of the old truths and offer biblical guidelines for the concerned father. It also offers some common sense. But especially it offers the hope that when Bible truths are obeyed regarding child rearing, the child "will not depart" from his father's faith when he is old.

Live as if You Are Being Followed

A small boy was trying to follow in his father's footsteps by literally placing his feet in the imprints left by his father's boots. The stride of his father, moving a few feet in front of the boy, was a little too long for the boy's legs to reach. After failing several times to reach his father's next footprint, the boy stopped and said, "Daddy, you're going to have to walk littler if you expect me to keep up."

It is good for fathers to walk "littler." When we act like men, think like men, speak like men, then men can relate to us and understand us. But small boys and girls cannot. Occasionally little boys and girls need fathers to become "little" again so that they can more easily follow. A wise father will take his lofty and noble ideals and reduce them into child-size goals.

One father told of a regimented program he attempted to initiate. He had attended a seminar that stressed the value of memorization, and he was determined to instill it in his family. He insisted on his children memorizing a chapter of the Bible each week. They complied for the first few weeks, and by then they had memorized their favorite chapters and the stress of having to memorize unfamiliar passages was becoming tiresome. Friends were playing ball games in the street. Others were telephoning just to talk, but they had no time to talk or play; they were struggling to memorize verses so that they could pass their father's "test."

When the stress finally erupted in an argument, the children made comments in their anger that they really did not mean, but once spoken words are impossible to retrieve. The father developed the damaging opinion, after the experiment in memorization failed, that his family was somehow lazier, inferior to other families. The truth was that he was taking awfully big steps for little children to follow.

The children in his home had very little of his own discipline, simply due to age and need. The father was accustomed to rising at an early hour in order to work all day at a job he was not always enamored with. The children were accustomed to sleeping until someone awakened them, and sometimes that took three or four attempts. There was nothing wrong with trying to develop a memory of verses. The goal was worthy, but the method and the demands were too much. Smaller steps, like memorizing a few short verses or playing a game of memory with the whole family, a means of showing the value of memorizing verses, would have been within their reach and probably would have had longer-lasting, positive results.

A father was afraid that his teenagers were missing biblical principles. He didn't know what to do about it. He took them to Sunday school, but he could only hope their teachers were doing a good job. He had tried to teach a few devotionals at home to his family, but he always felt stiff and unnatural doing so.

Then one day he struck on an idea. He placed a Bible on the table when the family gathered for their evening meal. As the meal began, he opened to Proverbs and read a couple of verses. He had deliberately chosen verses that had a "hidden" meaning. After reading them aloud, he asked his wife and children what they thought the verses meant. His manner was not that of preaching a sermon to his family. He was not putting on a sudden air of soberness. He was admitting to his family that he had not understood a couple of verses and was asking for their opinion.

This, of course, subtly revealed to his children that he had been reading the Bible somewhere besides at church. It also included them in a discussion of the verses under the guidance of the parents. The teenagers wanted to give their opinion and did so eagerly. The entire mealtime was passed in the discussion of what these verses might mean to a Christian today.

The mealtime Proverbs became an enjoyable pastime at many meals. It was not so large a step that the teens could not match it. It did not require them to be scholars. But it was a step, if only a step, in the direction the father wanted them to go—understanding and appreciating the principles the Bible teaches.

Lead Them, Don't Shove Them

A father and son were exploring a cave. The father's flashlight went on the blink, and so he stepped in behind his son and followed him for a while. Then they came to a bend in the dark cave, and the boy was hesitant as he felt his way around some boulders. At one point, he stopped moving and slipped around behind his father. Before his father even knew what he was doing, he put the flashlight in his dad's hand.

"What are you doing?" chuckled the father. The boy replied, "Well, you've been shoving me ever since your flashlight went out. You take the light and lead for a while; I'll shove."

Fathers should "take the light and lead" the child. The child does not profit from the father who is always telling him or her how to act or how not to act yet never showing by example just what he means. A father who tells his son to be a gentleman is teaching a good thing. Now let the father open the door for his wife. Let him also treat his own mother with courtesy. Thus by watching his father's lead the boy will follow more easily. His progress through this world will be much smoother if he can simply follow behind someone's sure lead rather than having to take the lead with someone behind shoving him.

The importance of a role model cannot be overstated. Psychologists today agree that one of the greatest factors in the destruction of moral value is the example of immorality continually portrayed in front of the children of today. Divorce has become so common that one public school teacher told her pastor that in her sixth grade class not one of her students was living with both his or her real mother and father. Every student in her class of thirty had suffered a divorce between his or her parents.

Today's parents say that they want the best for their children. The best gift a parent can give his child is a solid example of Christian living. The old adage, "I'd rather see a sermon than hear one," is a great truth. Children need to see a sermon. They get a lot of yelling from impatient parents. They get lots of correction. They do not need to be shoved into the mold. They need to be so impressed with their father's life and their mother's life that they want to get in the same mold.

A mother knelt beside her little boy's bed to hear his nighttime prayers. In typical nighttime conversation she asked what he would like to be when he grew up. His reply was, "I want to be just like my daddy." He did not name a career. He was not thinking about the kind of job his dad performed. He just wanted to be like his daddy.

One father confessed that he had been lazy about his religious habits. He would miss church on Sunday because the lawn needed mowing. He would not attend midweek Bible study class because he needed to balance the checkbook. Then one day he realized that he had a ten-year-old son who was in the other room arguing with his mother that he did not have to go to church on Sunday. He wanted to be like his father, he told her. The father was troubled to realize the boy's perception of him. In the father's mind, he was a good Christian who just missed church now and then. In the boy's mind, he was a man who did not have to go to church like other people did. After that experience the father made up his mind to live in such a way that he would be glad if his son copied him, leading him instead of ordering him.

Every father should live as if he knew his son or daughter would copy him. If he would be upset if his son cheated at school, then he must not cheat at home. If he would be upset if his daughter cursed and swore because she was angry, then he must not ever curse at home because he is angry.

Fathers are synonymous with authority and rules. The father who lays down the law at home, but then exempts himself from it, is foolish if he believes his children will obey his law and ignore his example. They will instead ignore his law and copy his example.

Before You Teach, Learn

The father must accept the responsibility of teaching his children. Too many fathers leave such matters to the mother, and while she may do a fine job, much is lost in the development of the child if he or she gains all religious instruction from the mother. Many a child has a subconscious perception that religion is more vital to women than to men. Many boys perceive submission to Christ as a weakness, not a strength. Such a perception comes from a father who does not assert himself as a Christian teacher.

The father who accepts his role as teacher to his children faces the task of what to teach and how to teach it. The first concern for the new father is what to learn. Before he can teach anything, he must learn.

Learn from Bible Role Models

None of God's great men divorced their wives. Therefore the father today should make up his mind that he will not divorce. He will live up to his vow, "Till death do us part." He will remember that he promised to "love, honor, and cherish" his wife. Avoiding divorce is not enough. He must continue to love her.

None of God's great men ever abused their children. To the contrary, we see David's example of loyalty and love to Absalom. Absalom had shamed his father, David, in front of all Israel. Yet when David sent his soldiers out to capture Absalom, he said, "Deal gently with the young man."

When the news of Absalom's death was brought to David, he wept and wailed, crying, "Absalom, my son, would God I had died for thee." Let a father make up his mind that right behind loving his wife "till death do us part" comes the urgent goal of saving his children. They are more important than career opportunities. They are more valuable than new houses.

None of God's great men neglected the temple or worship of God. To the contrary, they were devoted to it. Joshua's leadership epitomized them all when he said, "As for me and my house, we will serve the LORD" (Joshua 24:15). Moses chose to suffer affliction with God's people rather than to enjoy the riches of Egypt (Hebrews 11:25). David felt ashamed that he had a fine palace to live in but God did not have a fine temple, and so he amassed the supplies and the material which would make the building of a grand temple possible under his son's reign.

Let the wise father show his family that he believes in the importance of having a church to go to, to take a family to, to hear the Word of God preached. He shows them by faithful attendance, by tithing faithfully, and by making it a priority over other activities.

Learn Your Audience

No effective teacher would attempt to teach a lesson without first asking who will make up his audience. One young minister was invited to speak at a conference. He prepared his best sermon, imagining all the important men who would be there. He was grateful for the opportunity to preach in front of his peers, and especially in front of men who were his elders, men whom he knew only by name at the time. He arrived at the conference, thoroughly prepared. He picked up his welcome package and scanned the brochure for his name. It was not there. He experienced a mild panic as he read more thoroughly. The main service agenda did not have his name!

Then off on the right side of the brochure he saw the heading "Simultaneous Children's Classes." Sure enough, there was his name. He was teaching a child's class that night in an anteroom while in the auditorium another speaker was addressing the conference constituents. Later he discovered he had not read his invitation letter carefully.

For all he tried, he could not adapt his sermon to fit an audience of children. He was well-prepared, but for the wrong audience.

Some fathers have great knowledge but do not adapt their methods to fit their audience. If one has young children, he need not expect them to listen to his lectures just because he is their father. He will have to get on his audience's level, playing games, being funny, using less vocabulary, if he expects to get anything across.

One father had done very well as his children grew. They were conditioned for a one-night-a-week Bible study in their own home. Every Thursday night the father and his wife and children would sit down and study some subject in the Bible together. They would discuss and he would finally resolve any issues and make the final comments.

As time progressed and they grew older, he noticed more often the look of boredom on their faces. He tried to enliven his tone of voice, he tried never to be dull. Still it was difficult to interest them all the time. By the time his oldest daughter was in the eighth grade, he knew she was simply tolerating the family's weekly class.

He inwardly blamed the school, society, the age in which we live, and anything else he could think of. But finally he realized that blaming people or the times did not cure the problem. So he began to pray about some way to make his home Bible study more important and meaningful to his children.

He started observing the girls at play. One thing they enjoyed playing most was school. That puzzled him, because he thought their family Bible class had always kept a definite educational tone to it. It occurred to him that it was not playing school that was fun for them, but it was playing teacher! Each of them argued over who would get to be the teacher in their game.

So at the next family Bible study night he made this announcement: "Beginning next week, your mother and I are going to see how much you know, and how much you can teach us. Starting next week, you will each have a turn at teaching us. We will be your class. I have some posters and charts here which you can look through and use if you choose. You will take turns, the oldest teaching first. If you need help preparing your lesson, you can ask your mother or me, but the class is all yours, and we want to learn."

The children got excited about this, and for several months every weekly devotion was a fun, exciting class. The other children even listened with more rapt attention when it was one of their own doing the teaching. And studying to teach a lesson taught the children far more than they were learning from their father's lessons.

A father should study his children. What relates to sons may not relate to daughters. His approach to his children will vary according to their ages, their sex, their interests, and their physical and mental abilities.

Sharing Knowledge

Teaching is sharing. When a father begins to think of himself as a teacher, he often thinks of the most familiar setting involving teaching: the classroom. The child may not always respond well to the classroom format because he is bored with school, or upset over the pressure of testing and so on. Therefore, a wise father will learn to think of teaching in formats other than lecturing.

If he thinks of teaching as sharing his knowledge with his children, then he will likely be more creative in finding ways to "share" than he will to "teach" and will probably achieve much better results.

A mother can sit her daughters down and tell them how to mix ingredients, how to use the oven, how to ice a cake. Or she can convince her daughters to help her bake a surprise cake for their father's birthday. In doing so, the girls have a fun time of working with their mother, and they also learn how to mix ingredients, how to use the oven, how to clean up, and how to do something nice for someone else. All those lessons learned and no "teacher" in sight.

So a father can learn ways to involve his children in healthy, wholesome projects, sharing his knowledge and skills with them in pursuit of a common goal. They will learn much, and do so without a "teacher."

Involve children in helping another family. Almost every church has a list of some families who need clothing, food, or other things. A father who wants to teach his children about Christian service to others can do no better than to find such a family and "adopt" them. If helping the other family becomes his own family's project, his children are going to learn a lot about "giving a cup of cold water in Jesus' name," and yet they may not even know where the verse is found.

Explain reasons more than you give orders. When Moses was leading the children of Israel out of bondage, the Lord instructed him to teach the fathers of Israel that when the day came that their sons came to them and asked a reason for the statutes they observed they were to respond properly. The fathers were to say, "We were in bondage, but God set us free." (See Deuteronomy 6:20-25.) In other words, first, in their infancy, the fathers had made the children obey certain religious laws. But all children come to an age where they must know why they are doing such things. Rather than bluntly inform inquisitive children that they had just better obey or else, Moses taught fathers to teach their children about the past.

A modern application of such principles might go something like this. A son comes to his father who has never smoked tobacco and never allowed his children to and asks, "Why can't I smoke? What's wrong with smoking?" The father can respond in one or more of three typical ways: (1) He can explain the physical harm of smoking and encourage the boy to better health; (2) He can tell the boy that he cannot smoke because "I said you can't, and that's that." No arguments allowed; or (3) He can tell the boy that he can smoke, but that he should know that there are a lot of people who wish they had never started smoking, people who would give anything to reverse the curse of cancer caused from smoking but they cannot seem to find a deliverer. As for this father, he too could smoke if he chose, but once Jesus the deliverer came to give him the power to overcome the bondage of tobacco and the liberty to choose life, he chose liberty. He could curse, and perhaps did at one time, but then Jesus came and gave him the power not to curse. Jesus delivered him from the weakness of the ordinary man. Therefore, while he could curse, he isn't bound to cursing. He is free from it.

Be a Friend

Children will learn more quickly if they like their teacher. A daughter came home from the first day of school. "How did it go?" her father asked. "Great!" she replied, "except for algebra!"

"What happened in algebra?" he asked.

"Nothing," she said. "It's just that I can't stand the teacher in there. I like my English teacher, my history teacher, and my science teacher, but I can't stand my algebra teacher." For some reason, the algebra teacher had made a negative impression on her, and the father knew that if his daughter struggled in any class, it would be in algebra. Sure enough, every six weeks it was algebra that evoked the worst groans and biggest arguments. Her father tried to motivate her to more diligent study, but it was fruitless. Her mind was set; she hated algebra. In truth, all of us are more likely to pick up a new subject if we like the person who is teaching us.

A Christian father found out that his son was smoking. He knew it was because of the influence of his high school friends, but he did not want to drive his son further from him by harshness. That would only cause his son to become more secretive about his behavior. The father went to his pastor, who gave him a strong challenge: "Say nothing about the smoking; spend more time with your son doing whatever the two of you can do together. Become best friends."

It was slow getting started. He had to make up projects for them to do, and sometimes they just did not work. Several times he smelled smoke in his son's clothing, and he wanted to chastise him, but he managed to remain quiet. After a couple of weeks, it was not so difficult for him to think of things they could do together—ordinary things. Instead of trying to make up big activities for them to do, he learned how to do the simple, everyday tasks with his son.

They washed the car together. Where the father used to come in from work and hit the recliner, fussing about not being able to get any work out of his kids, he now came in, changed clothes, threw a towel in his son's hands and went out the door saying, "Come on, let's wash and wax your car."

A surprised son followed cautiously at first, but there were no strings attached. They washed, buffed tires, and waxed. They repaired little things that did not work any more—not on the family car, but on the son's car. The more the father got involved in his son's life, the more the son responded favorably. Soon, if the father was sitting in the garage about to clean his tools, the son would say, "Need any help?" And the father would pitch him a brush, and the two of them would work away.

Gradually, the son learned that a man does not have to smoke to be a man. He was learning that his father was a great guy, and he did not have to smoke to prove it.

Most of the time children try new things because they are impressed by the person who offers them the new experience more than they are intrigued by the experience itself. When sons and daughters become impressed with their father's friendship, they are less likely to be impressed with other kids who do not measure up to their dad.

Be an Example of Prayer

It is one thing to tell children to pray. It is better to simply be a man of prayer.

It is very simple to know what to pray.

Pray for yourself. A father needs to pray for himself, asking God for wisdom to know how to be a good Christian father. As he prays, he can ask God to give him insight into the problems and trials of his children and the ability to assist them from his vantage point of greater knowledge and experience. Experience that can profit someone else is invaluable.

Pray for your children. A father should pray for his children, asking God to spare them from evil men. He needs to ask God to keep their hearts pure, to help them learn to make good choices, and to save them.

The responsibility of leading children to Jesus Christ lies in the hands of the parent. Parents who ignore their spiritual responsibility to the child while attending to their social, financial, and physical responsibilities are usually headed for a sad awakening. They will likely be lost if their salvation has not been a matter of importance to the parents.

Pray for all those who touch the lives of your children. Fathers can pray for their children's teachers at school. By getting to know them and by getting involved in parent-teacher organizations, the father will let them see that he is a concerned, loving, and Christian parent.

A father also needs to pray for his children's Sunday school teachers, youth leaders in the church, and his pastor. He should pray that every message they hear will be godly and soul-strengthening.

Allow them to see and hear you pray. A father should not be as a Pharisee and pray just so his children will see. But neither should he hide his prayer life from his family. It is true that we are to enter "into our closets and pray in secret." But if children never see or hear us pray, they will miss this example in developing their own communication with God. They need the example. At least once a week, if at all possible, a father should invite his family to join him in praying for specific people and specific causes. In such praying he will demonstrate worship of God, care for others, his faith in the power of prayer to change things, and his example of praying.

A father must accept that God has placed in his hands the responsibility of training and equipping his children for spiritual maturity. He must live as if he is being followed, for he certainly is. He must realize that he cannot simply tell his children what they must do but he must lead them by being an example of his instructions. He should learn from the great men the Bible gives us for our own examples, he must learn about his own children, and he must adapt his teaching according to their ages, sex, skills, interests, and physical and mental abilities.

A Christian father must be a man of prayer. He should pray for himself to be what God wants him to be, for his children to be saved, and for everyone who touches the lives of his children.

Test Your Knowledge

True and False

_____1. Another concept of teaching is sharing.

_____2. A father should not try to be a friend to his children but rather display a rigid example of strength.

_____3. Fathers should think of leading their children more than of telling or shoving them.

_____4. A father has the power to make Bible reading a part of the family's normal routine.

_____5. Fathers should deal with giving reasons more than with giving orders.

Apply Your Knowledge

Find a way to turn the family meal into a fun discussion of a Bible principle. Read a proverb that has direct application to the lives of your children or to your own life, and get your family involved in a helpful discussion of it.

Make up your mind to be your children's best friend. You will have to get on their level to do so, but the trip will be well worth the effort.

Expand Your Knowledge

An excellent book worth reading by parents is entitled *The Blessing* by Gary Smalley and John Trent, Ph.D., published by Thomas Nelson Publishers. It is available from the Pentecostal Publishing House, 8855 Dunn Road, Hazelwood, MO 63042-2299.

Marriage— I Found a Good Thing

8

Whoso findeth a wife findeth a good thing, and obtaineth favour of the LORD.

Proverbs 18:22

Start With the Scriptures

Genesis 2:18-24;
24:61-67

John 2:1-11
Hebrews 13:4

While marriage is practiced in every society of the world and finds its roots in the most ancient history, some have suggested that it is merely a human institution which has failed and deserves abandonment. Perhaps one of the most radical statements ever published appeared in *The Document: a declaration of feminism:*

"All of history must be rewritten in terms of the oppression of women.... Marriage has existed for the benefit of men and has been a legally sanctioned method of control over women. . . . The end of the institution of marriage is a necessary condition for the liberation of women. Therefore, it is important for us to encourage women to leave their husbands and not to live individually with men. . . . Now we know it is the institution that has failed us and we must work to destroy it. . . ."

Is marriage simply a social phenomenon? Would another structure be superior? The Holy Scriptures give a negative answer to both questions. Marriage is God's idea, and it will never be replaced regardless of the desperate efforts of misguided radicals.

The Origin of Marriage

In the eyes of God, all of His original creation was good (Genesis 1:4, 10, 12, 18, 21, 25). But when God created man, the apex of all God's work, He said, "It is not good . . ." (Genesis 2:18). What was it that was not good about man's creation? God said, "It is not good that the man should be alone; I will make him an help meet for him" (Genesis 2:18).

So marriage is not man's idea. It will never be replaced as long as the earth stands, for marriage provides companionship for humans and is God's plan for the perpetuation of humanity. Thousands of years after creation, Solomon said, "Whoso findeth a wife findeth a good thing, and obtaineth favour of the LORD" (Proverbs 18:22).

The original statement on marriage, which is repeated three times in the New Testament, sums up the purpose and intent of God in creating the woman for the man. "Therefore shall a man leave his father and his mother, and shall cleave unto his wife: and they shall be one flesh" (Genesis 2:24).

With every marriage, a new family structure is created. While a man continues to honor his mother and father, in marriage he cleaves to his wife and the two of them become one flesh. No longer are they considered merely as separate individuals. They have actually added a new dimension to their identity.

Jesus, commenting on this original plan, said, "Wherefore they are no more twain, but one flesh. What therefore God hath joined together, let not man put asunder" (Matthew 19:6).

Clearly, the plan of God for marriage is simple: one man and one woman for life.

Isaac and Rebekah

One of the most beautiful and inspiring stories of married love is that of Isaac and Rebekah. (See Genesis 24:61-67.) The providence of God is seen in bringing these two together. In this case, God had a specific man and woman for each other.

As Isaac meditated in the field in the evening, he looked up and saw the camel train of his father Abraham's servant returning. Rebekah accompanied the train. Isaac took her to his mother's tent, she became his wife, and his love for her comforted Isaac following his mother's death.

It is significant that Abraham did not want Isaac to take a wife from among the Canaanites (Genesis 24:3). He asked his servant to swear before God to bring Isaac a wife from Abraham's country and kindred (Genesis 24:4).

Later, the Lord would command the people of Israel not to make marriages with the heathen (Deuteronomy 7:1-3). There can be no doubt as to the purpose of this command: God did not want His people corrupted by the influence of wives and mothers who worshiped false gods.

Marriage, an Honorable Institution

It should come as no surprise to see Satan's attack on marriage. He is against everything that is good, honorable, and of God. For this reason he tempts both men and women to be unfaithful to marriage vows, to enter into physical relationships without the benefit of marriage, and in general to ridicule the concept of marriage as a good, holy thing.

The writer of Hebrews declared: "Marriage is honourable in all, and the bed undefiled: but whoremongers and adulterers God will judge" (Hebrews 13:4). Marriage is honorable. It is not to be the brunt of jokes. It is certainly not a necessary evil to legitimize lust and to provide tax breaks.

Jesus' presence at the marriage in Cana illustrates well the importance of this institution in the eyes of God. (See John 2:1-11.)

Jesus' presence at the wedding revealed not only His miracle-working power, but also His interest in the happiness of people. The fact that His first miracle was that of saving the host from embarrassment by turning water into a wine even finer than that which had been served at the first shows us His interest in man's happiness and specifically in the institution of marriage.

Many spiritual leaders of our day would think their time far too valuable to spend helping a newly married couple rejoice. But Jesus was interested in the things that really mattered. And He knew that marriage is the basic foundation of society and therefore an important institution that predates even the church on earth.

Seducing Spirits

Paul warned Timothy that in the last days, among other things, seducing spirits teaching devilish doctrines would forbid marriage (I Timothy 4:1-3). The lie taught by these spirits is that marriage is an inferior state. The subtle suggestion is planted: the married life reduces spirituality and loads one down with the unnecessary baggage of family responsibilities.

This lie historically became incorporated in some religious movements which forbid marriage to their spiritual leaders. Today it is found in cults that discourage marriage by demanding total submission to a dictatorial leader. It is also found among those who hold the "social purity" doctrine, which permits marriage but commands the husband and wife to live as brother and sister.

The Word of God is clear on the subject of marriage:
- It is not good that man should be alone.
- He who finds a wife finds a good thing and obtains favor of God.
- Marriage is honorable in all.
- The marriage relationship represents the relationship between Christ and the church (Ephesians 5:22-23).

What about Paul's comments in I Corinthians 7? Did he not say, "For I would that all men were even as I myself" (I Corinthians 7:7)? And did he not say, "Art thou loosed from a wife? seek not a wife" (I Corinthians 7:27)? And what about the statement, "He that is unmarried careth for the things that belong to the Lord, how he may please the Lord: But he that is married careth for the things that are of the world, how he may please his wife" (I Corinthians 7:32-33)?

Paul wrote these statements; however, it is essential in interpreting these verses to start from the context of all of the Scriptures on this subject, narrow its focus down to the context of the New Testament, then to the other writings of Paul himself, and finally to the context of the chapter.

First, we note that marriage is never spoken of in a negative way in the Word of God. Every statement about it is positive.

Second, Jesus endorsed marriage by His personal presence in Cana and by His reference to Genesis 2.

Third, Paul himself endorsed marriage, gave instructions for wives and husbands, and declared that marriage symbolized the relationship between Christ and the chruch.

What, then, do his statements in I Corinthians 7 mean?

The key verse in understanding Paul's statements about marriage in this chapter is I Corinthians 7:26: "I suppose therefore that this is good for the present distress, I say, that it is good for a man so to be." The thought that tempered all of Paul's statements on marriage in this chapter was *this present distress.* Either the church was then experiencing unusual persecution and pressure or it soon would be. While it was permissible to marry, even in this situation ["But and if thou marry, thou hast not sinned . . ." (verse 28)], marriage would bring on additional pressures in a day that was extremely difficult already.

For example, it is one thing for a single individual to face martyrdom for his faith; it is quite another for a husband and father to think about the care of his family.

It is certainly possible that the circumstances at Corinth could be repeated today. There could be times and places where persecution is so intense that it would be better for those who are single to remain in that state, at least until the pressure has passed.

Continuing his comments on the fact that marriage is permissible, though perhaps not advisable, Paul said, "Nevertheless such [as go ahead and marry] shall have trouble in the flesh: but I spare you" (I Corinthians 7:28). In most times and places, however, marriage is not only permissible—it is encouraged. Husband and wife complete a unit socially, provide companionship for both, and form the social institution for children, who are the heritage of the Lord (I Corinthians 11:9; Psalm 127:3).

How to Treat Your Wife

Peter, a married man, said husbands should give "honour unto the wife, as unto the weaker vessel" (I Peter 3:7). In what way is a wife the "weaker vessel"? Surely this is not describing physical, emotional, or spiritual weakness.

While on average men are physically stronger than women, there seems to be a more important basis to Peter's statement than comparative physical strength. Besides, women are strong and in some cases are physically stronger than their husbands!

It is difficult to imagine that women are emotionally or spiritually weaker than men because, while they may express themselves differently, they too are made in the image of God.

It seems best to understand Peter's statement as referring not to an inferior, weak vessel, but to a fragile, exquisite vessel, like an expensive vase. A fragile vase may not be physically as tough as a simple glass vase from the variety store, but it is much more beautiful and valuable.

Men, in other words, should treat their wives like a person would handle a very rare, beautiful, and valuable work of art. What is involved in this?

A man should respect his wife. A man must never belittle or demean his wife. He should respect her for the following reasons:

- She is a unique human being, made in the image of God (Genesis 1:27).
- She completes what is lacking in the man (Genesis 2:18).
- She is her husband's glory (I Corinthians 11:7).
- Every man since Adam is made of a woman, including the Son of God (I Corinthians 11:11; Galatians 4:4).

- The marriage symbolizes the relationship between Christ and the church (Ephesians 5:22-33).
- In Christ Jesus there is neither male nor female (Galatians 3:28).
- The value of a virtuous woman is far above rubies (Proverbs 31:10).
- A virtuous woman is worthy of praise (Proverbs 31:28).

The man who respects his wife finds that she responds favorably to him. The more critical and condemning he is, the further the gap between them grows.

A part of a man's respect for his wife involves his encouragement for her to develop her God-given talents and gifts. If there is a project or hobby she enjoys, he should admire her efforts, show interest in her progress, and encourage her to reach her goals.

A man should honor his wife. Honor is an attitude. A man need not always agree with his wife on every subject to honor her. It would be strange indeed for a husband and wife to agree on every issue. We are, after all, unique individuals.

But a wise husband will express to his wife his deep appreciation for her. He may do this with thoughtfully chosen cards or flowers. And he will not limit these expressions to birthdays, anniversaries, and other holidays.

A wise husband will also from time to time let his wife overhear him praising her to another person. When a wife hears her husband expressing his admiration for her to another, it encourages and strengthens her. Ephesians 4:29 admonishes: "Let no corrupt communication proceed out of your mouth, but that which is good to the use of edifying, that it may minister grace unto the hearers."

A man should love his wife. While there will be

strong emotional attachments between a man and his wife, love is more than an emotion or feeling. Love is a decision. The Bible does not recognize as valid the portrayal of love given by Hollywood and cheap romance novels.

Men are commanded to love their wives and to demonstrate that love in the same way Christ demonstrated His love for the church (Ephesians 5:25). Love is defined in I Corinthians 13:4-7.

For a man to say, "I no longer love my wife," is an act of rebellion against God and a failure to understand the meaning of love. Redefining love as an ethereal feeling with its focus on self-centered sensual and emotional fulfillment is not only selfish but also sinful.

A man who decides to have eyes for his wife only (Job 31:1) and to focus his human affections only on her (Proverbs 5:15-20) finds genuine love growing ever greater with the passing years. This love is satisfying and fulfilling, as opposed to sensual lust, which often passes for love and which leaves both its victims frustrated and sad.

Make Your Wife Feel Special

A husband should think creatively about how to do things that will make his wife feel special to him. They could plan special days together when just the two of them will enjoy a drive through scenic countryside, a dinner in a quaint restaurant, or just an evening talking. These times should be planned, because a wife enjoys the anticipation as well as the actual event. She will also enjoy the memories of time together.

But special times should not wait until it is possible to take a whole day together. A man can provide enjoyable and refreshing time with his wife by sharing special moments during the day. An unexpected telephone call, a card in the mail, lunch together at a mutually agreed upon restaurant—all of these and many other simple things make a wife feel special.

A woman wants to be a part of her husband's world. He should freely tell her about his work, his dreams, his thoughts. And he should be willing to listen to her descriptions of her day and to encourage her in her goals in life.

Your Marriage Can Succeed

Contrary to the propaganda of humanists and feminists, marriage can not only work but also be a blessed and enjoyable relationship between two people who have great respect and admiration for each other. There are, however, some simple requirements for this to happen.

You must be willing to work at your marriage. A successful marriage does not just happen. It requires effort, study, trial and error. You must never entertain the thought that divorce might be a solution—in the eyes of God, it never is. The solution to every problem is available through the grace of God and the Word of God.

Marriage will succeed at its best only for those who have a firm, unswerving commitment to the success of their marriage and who refuse to be turned from that commitment by the alluring voices of compromise.

You must be willing to change. In order for a marriage to succeed at its best, both partners must be willing to do some changing. It is impossible to anticipate in advance of marriage all of the changes that will be necessary. Each partner will disagree with some behavior of the other as he gets to know the other better.

The realities of married life are always divergent

from the mental pictures both parties painted before marriage. Unwillingness to change to accommodate or please one's partner is a sign of immaturity and a sure formula for marital disaster.

You must have high dreams. Marriage must not be allowed to stagnate into a dreary sameness. No one is happy and fulfilled who is not achieving and growing. There must always be something to look forward to.

While God often allows two totally different personality types to come together in marriage, it should be possible for the husband and wife to sit down and together work out short and long-range goals in life. What role do they want to play in their children's education? When do they plan to purchase a home? What about a new car? What are their spiritual goals? What projects can they complete together?

Though Paul accomplished many things in his life, he wrote: "Brethren, I count not myself to have apprehended: but this one thing I do, forgetting those things which are behind, and reaching forth unto those things which are before, I press toward the mark for the prize of the high calling of God in Christ Jesus" (Philippians 3:13-14).

As a married couple moves through the various phases of life—newlyweds, childbearing, childrearing, marriage of children, grandchildren—they must always be able to look forward to new and higher goals they will reach for together.

Test Your Knowledge

1. Why is marriage under attack?
2. What was not good about man's creation?
3. List two reasons why, as a rule, the married state is superior to the single state.

4. Explain Paul's reservations about marriage in I Corinthians 7.

5. What did Peter mean when he referred to the wife as "the weaker vessel"?

Apply Your Knowledge

It is time now to *do* something to improve and strengthen your relationship with your wife. Ask yourself these questions:

1. When was the last time I brought my wife a flower?

2. When was the last time I told my wife I loved her and was really thinking about what I was saying?

3. Do I make critical remarks which demean my wife?

4. If someone asked my wife about our relationship, how would she describe it?

5. When is the nearest time in the future that my wife and I can share a special day together, alone?

6. What one thing can I change about myself that would make my wife grateful?

7. What goals have we set together?

Expand Your Knowledge

Ask your wife to write down three things she would like to see happen in your marriage. Take the list, without excuses or criticism, and prayerfully begin to seek God for ways to fulfill your wife's wishes.

Locate and read Gary Smalley's book, *If Only He Knew* (Grand Rapids, MI: Zondervan, 1982).

Read James Dobson's book, *What Wives Wish Their Husbands Knew About Women* (Tyndale, 1977).

Morality – Take the High Road

9

Create in me a clean heart, O God; and renew a right spirit within me.

Psalm 51:10

Start With the Scriptures

Genesis 39
Psalm 51:1-19

Isaiah 6:1-7

Perhaps the single greatest flaw in humanity since the fall in Eden is man's selfish insistence that he can determine what is moral and what is not. Unfortunately, depraved mankind is incapable of establishing sound moral principles in his personal life or in society. At the same time, he suffers from guilt that comes from a God-given, innate sense of right and wrong.

Regardless of the efforts through the centuries to establish a utopian society, mankind has not progressed beyond his innate sinfulness. Today, we are not far removed from the social and spiritual evil that permeated the people in the days of Noah: "the wickedness of man was great ... and ... the thoughts of his heart was only evil continually" (Genesis 6:5). We sometimes fail to clearly recognize the disastrous plunge in personal values among people of every social level and the accompanying confusion that moral failure causes in the family.

A wise man once said, "If we do not learn from our mistakes, we are doomed to repeat them." And repeating them, we are!

An examination of biblical history yields many examples of the dire consequences that result when men and nations lose their moral balance, electing to do that which was right in their own eyes (Judges 17:6). Secular history has tragic examples of vast political empires that, after establishing noteworthy institutions and achieving great knowledge and skills, fell into chaos and ruins. One basic cause for failure was the abandonment of moral teachings upon which their success had been founded.

Married couples, singles, and young people alike are struggling with the confusing signals that are coming from a variety of television and radio media, social activists, and religious leaders. These many voices, both in and out of religious circles, have declared the old morality of the past to be obsolete in today's "enlightened, high tech" society.

Individualism is the byword of the day. Some have been so bold as to state that it is the individual, not God or His Word, that should be the final judge of what is moral or immoral. They adopt a vain philosophy of self-indulgence designed to appease a constant appetite for pleasure. Their basic doctrine is instant self-gratification. They counsel, "If you want it, then you can have it." And through such carnal reasoning, they endorse and encourage the individual to sacrifice his personal character and integrity on the altar of selfish desires.

Society's loss of its moral and spiritual equilibrium has given rise to the conclusion that today's men and women have become "lovers of pleasures more than lovers of God." (See II Timothy 3.) In the process, irreparable spiritual and emotional damage has been done to countless relationships, fragile marriages, and family units. Once the tragic seed of immorality has been sown, the bitter fruit of heartache, ruined reputations, and broken lives will be reaped.

In such a confused social atmosphere, the Christian man, married or single, must find the spiritual courage to demonstrate the highest quality of morality and standards of conduct. He must not only provide moral leadership for his own family but also lead by example in his church, his neighborhood, and his workplace. There is only one road here for the Christian man to take—the high road!

A Discouraging Moral Climate

Recent surveys of college students at several universities indicate that many students do not share the belief that moral principles expressed in God's Word are significant. One survey revealed that sixty-seven percent of the male students and fifty-two percent of the faculty members stated that moral values were not a major consideration in their daily behavioral patterns. In fact, the majority of both student and faculty men stated that strict adherence to high principles of morality would place them at an unacceptable disadvantage when competing for jobs, business opportunities, and personal relationships with women. Fifty-eight percent of the male students and forty-nine percent of the male faculty members stated that sexual purity before marriage was an unrealistic expectation, and that sexual fidelity during marriage was an outmoded idea that is probably not desirable in today's liberal atmosphere.

Perhaps the most shocking fact is that fully forty-five percent of the male faculty members endorsed both male and female homosexual relationships as a viable alternative to conventional marriage between the sexes. These faculty members are the instructors who influence the personal beliefs, ethics, and moral values of today's young adults.

The Well-traveled Low Road

The battle for moral integrity and sexual purity is not restricted to the university campus. Everyone is exposed to the never-ending sexual propaganda and subtle images permeating our daily lives through the multifaceted media. We are constantly inundated by recurring sexual themes in radio, television, billboard, and magazine advertisements, as well as the heavy doses of sexually explicit lyrics in some rock music and the raw language and nudity prevalent in some current motion pictures.

Sexual situations are often depicted between young, attractive, and unmarried adults. The message is unmistakable—sex, under any circumstance, with any partner, is quite permissible, even expected. The strong implication is that everyone is doing it, so why insist on being different?

Although the momentum of the so-called "sexual revolution" of the late sixties and early seventies has slowed somewhat in recent years, premarital and extramarital sexual relationships still happen at an alarming rate.

Disregarding the current AIDS phenomenon, other sexually transmitted diseases (gonorrhea, syphilis, herpes, etc.), which medical science has battled for centuries, have achieved epidemic proportions and are becoming increasingly more resistent to current medical treatment. Some strains have become immune to previously effective remedies. Such events seem to beg the question, "Doth not even nature itself teach you?" (I Corinthians 11:14).

High Morals and Purity

In order to properly conduct ourselves morally and ethically before the Lord, we must understand that it is God who has established the moral standards and values by which we are to live. It is true that men have altered the customs and traditions of nations and races, but high moral principles set by God are unchanging. Honesty, goodness, mercy, justice, sexual fidelity, and right behavior remain the basis upon which a society survives.

Because God is the author of moral truths given to us through His Word, moral precepts remain in force generation after generation. It is God's desire that every man present to Him "a clean heart and a right spirit." We are to live responsibly as moral beings before our God and before others.

God's High Expectations

Regardless of society's inability or refusal to establish high standards for personal morality and sexual purity, God's Word establishes His expectations for man's behavior and conduct. The Word of God is replete with admonitions and commands that address specific acts of immorality and condemn the sinfulness of evil thoughts such as lust, hate, and pride. (See Psalm 81:11-12; Matthew 5:27-28; Galatians 5:19; I Thessalonians 4:3-7; Titus 2:12-14; James 1:14-15; I Peter 2:11-12; I John 2:16.)

Knowing the pressures of sexual temptation, the

apostle Paul, under the anointing of the Holy Ghost, gave prudent advice to a young Christian pastor and friend, Timothy. Paul instructed Timothy to be "an example of the believers . . . in purity" (I Timothy 4:12). This purity was to be demonstrated in word and deed. Paul instructed Timothy to be especially sensitive to his relationships with women so that neither his words nor his actions could be misinterpreted. Paul continued, "Intreat . . . the elder women as mothers; the younger as sisters, with all purity . . . keep thyself pure" (I Timothy 5:1-2, 22). This wise counsel remains relevant today, and it must not be lost on our generation of young Christian men.

Clear Definitions

While the world regards personal sexual mores as a "gray" area to be determined by the individual, the Scriptures have confronted these issues in clear terms. The Holy Scriptures do not take a timid or vague approach to the subject of sexual immorality. Having sexual relations outside the confines of marriage is a violation of God's commandment, and therefore a sin.

Two particular categories of illicit sexual activity are most frequently referred to in discussions of sexual immorality. These are adultery and fornication. The word *adultery,* according to *Fausset's Bible Dictionary,* is defined as "sexual intercourse between a married person and someone other than his or her lawful spouse." Fornication, on the other hand, in biblical use, refers to all illicit sexual activity, including adultery; however, modern use of the term limits its meaning to sexual relations between unmarried partners. Both adultery and fornication are immoral acts condemned by God. Throughout the Bible, sexual sins, including homosexuality, incest, transexuality, and bestiality are explicitly condemned. (See Leviticus 18:5-25, 19:20-22, 20:10-21; Deuteronomy 22:5, 13-30; Romans 1:24-32; I Corinthians 6:9-20.)

Sowing and Reaping

In today's troubling moral climate, both premarital and extramarital sexual relationships have been depicted as glamorous, exciting experiences in which no one is hurt, no one is humiliated, and no one is emotionally scarred. The new moralists profess that illicit sex is simply a "victimless crime" causing no harm or injury to the consenting parties. But nothing could be further from the truth!

A recent survey of practicing clinical psychologists and psychiatrists indicates that illicit sex leaves ruined lives. Of those responding to the survey, eighty-eight percent stated that they had documented evidence of permanent emotional injury in patients who sought treatment as a direct result of their involvement in illicit sexual relationships. The most common symptoms were depression, loss of self-esteem and self-worth, bitterness, uncontrollable outbursts of emotion (violence, anger, and weeping), guilt, and chronic physical illness. Of the cases involving adultery, eighty-three percent of the marriages ended in divorce or extended separation. Sixty-two percent of the patients were men.

After its "false decorations" and "shiny wrappings" have been removed, illicit sex is exposed for what it really is—sin. Acts of adultery and fornication are gross sins and carry with them the heavy emotional penalty of immense guilt and mental anguish. The apostle James described immorality's progressive, downward spiral when he wrote, "Then when lust hath conceived, it bringeth forth sin: and sin, when it is finished, bringeth forth death" (James

1:15). His advice to the Christian man concerning fleshly lusts is uncomplicated—"Do not err, my beloved brethren" (James 1:16).

Live Morally Clean

As never before, there is a need for Christian men from every walk of life to live morally clean before their families and the world. The biblical commands for moral purity are unambiguous and are soundly supported by doctrinal instruction throughout the Word of God. The Scriptures reveal several reasons as to why moral purity is such an important characteristic of the Christian believer.

First, illicit sex is expressly prohibited. "Thou shalt not commit adultery" (Exodus 20:14; Deuteronomy 5:18). So serious was the offense of unchastity in patriarchal times that death by fire was the penalty (Genesis 38:24). Capital punishment also continued under the Mosaic law (Leviticus 20:10; Deuteronomy 22:22). In Matthew 19:18, Jesus upheld this Old Testament commandment in His conversation with the rich young ruler.

Both adultery and fornication, among other grievous sins, are specifically addressed in various New Testament references:

"For out of the heart proceed evil thoughts, murders, adulteries, fornications. . . . These are the things which defile a man" (Matthew 15:19-20).

"Be not deceived: neither fornicators, nor idolaters, nor adulterers, nor effeminate, nor abusers of themselves with mankind . . . shall inherit the kingdom of God" (I Corinthians 6:9-10).

"Now the works of the flesh are manifest, which are these; Adultery, fornication, uncleanness, lasciviousness. . . . They which do such things shall not inherit the kingdom of God" (Galatians 5:19-21).

Second, immorality will be severely punished.

From the sobering example of Sodom and Gomorrah's destruction to the apostle John's prophetic statements in the Book of Revelation, the Scriptures plainly indicate that sexual immorality brings the judgment and wrath of God. Not only are those who engage in illicit and perverted sexual practices barred from the kingdom of God (I Corinthians 6:9-10; Galatians 5:19-21), but just as Sodom and Gomorrah reaped the judgment of brimstone and fire (Genesis 19:24), so too will the whoremonger "have their part in the lake which burneth with fire and brimstone: which is the second death" (Revelation 21:8).

The apostle Paul reserved his strongest warning for those who would commit indecent and unnatural sexual sins (Colossians 3:6). He called them "children of disobedience" and said the wrath of God would come upon them. To the church at Rome, Paul further explained that "they which commit such things are worthy of death" (Romans 1:32).

Third, sins of immorality violate the marriage covenant. Genesis 2:24 declares that man and wife are to be "one flesh." Jesus affirmed this moral principle in the Gospels (Matthew 19:5; Mark 10:8) and the apostle Paul reinforced it again in his teachings to the church at Ephesus (Ephesians 5:31).

Paul referred to this violation of the sanctity of marriage in I Corinthians 6:16 when he asked, "What? know ye not that he which is joined to an harlot is one body? for two, saith he, shall be one flesh." When a man and woman commit adultery or fornication they come together as one flesh, a union that God sanctions only within the marriage relationship.

Fourth, our bodies are not our own; they are the temple of the Holy Ghost. Writing to the Corinthian church which had experienced a great deal of confusion because of sexual immorality, the apostle Paul instructed the church, "What? know ye not that your body is the temple of the Holy Ghost which is in you, which ye have of God, and ye are not your own? For ye are bought with a price" (I Corinthians 6:19-20). In verse 13, the admonition is direct: "Now the body is not for fornication, but for the Lord; and the Lord for the body." Our bodies are not ours to abuse and defile as we wish; they are God's. And as the temple of the Holy Ghost they must be kept clean and holy. (See I Corinthians 3:16-17.)

Sexuality Is God's Gift

The biblical commandments against sexual immorality do not imply a condemnation of natural and wholesome human sexuality. On the contrary, God created man and woman as sexual beings and intended that they enjoy an intimate sexual relationship within marriage. "Marriage is honourable in all, and the bed undefiled" (Hebrews 13:4).

Through physical intimacy, the married couple demonstrates their lifelong love, fidelity, and respect for each other. Procreation is not the only purpose of sex. It is also a beautiful gift of God for the pleasure and mutual enjoyment of both husband and wife. A happy and fulfilling sexual life is a wonderfully satisfying aspect of marriage when both partners are sensitive to one another's needs, work to improve the relationship, and give of themselves in a spirit of love, concern, and unselfishness.

A Call for Moral Men

Satan is bringing tremendous pressures to bear on Christian men today in an attempt to draw them into sexual immorality. He will use any means possible to entice good men to succumb to the temptations of sexual indulgence. A close, genuine relationship with God and a sensitivity to the leading of His Spirit are an absolute necessity in overcoming these powerful temptations. After all, "Greater is he that is in you, than he that is in the world" (I John 4:4).

Godly men, living morally clean and sexually pure in this present world provide one of the greatest testimonies to the overcoming power that is possible through the Holy Ghost. By placing ourselves completely in His hands we are able to present our bodies as a living sacrifice that is holy and acceptable to Him (Romans 12:1). The call to morality and purity is from the Lord; we must answer it and take the high road.

"Now unto him that is able to keep you from falling, and to present you faultless before the presence of his glory with exceeding joy, To the only wise God our Saviour, be glory and majesty, dominion and power, both now and ever. Amen" (Jude 24-25).

Test Your Knowledge

1. In your own words, describe the causes of today's dramatic moral decline.
2. How have the news and entertainment media influenced personal moral values?
3. Why are sound moral principles and sexual purity expected of every generation?
4. Describe the apostle Paul's admonition to Timothy concerning sexual purity.
5. Explain the differences in definition between adultery and fornication.
6. Are illicit sexual acts "victimless crimes"? Explain.
7. List four reasons for moral purity.
8. Are all sexual relationships condemned by the Scriptures? Explain.
9. How does adultery destroy the "one flesh" relationship between husband and wife?

10. What is the Christian man's best protection against sexual temptation?

Apply Your Knowledge

"Study to shew thyself approved unto God, a workman that needeth not to be ashamed" (II Timothy 2:15). Self-examination is always in order. Take a long, honest look at your personal moral values. Are they a reflection of the teachings and standards of the Word of God? Are your moral values consistent with your "real world" moral and sexual conduct?

Identify and acknowledge both your strengths and weaknesses in regard to personal moral behavior and sexual purity. Ask God to increase your spiritual strength, and determine to exemplify true, scriptural morality and a genuine Christian character in all aspects of everyday life.

Expand Your Knowledge

Consider a careful and detailed character study of King David. Pay particular attention to the origin, cause, individual actions, and final consequences of David's sexual sin with Bathsheba.

In addition, note especially the nature of David's personal response when confronted by the man of God about his immorality. The insights gained by such a character study will prove valuable in helping you to understand your own humanity, and it will also increase your trust in God's ability to sustain your personal walk with Him.

Be the Best You Can Be   10

For as he thinketh in his heart, so is he: Eat and drink, saith he to thee; but his heart is not with thee.
Proverbs 23:7

Start With the Scriptures

Romans 8:36-39
Philippians 4:8
I Timothy 6:1-21

Man was created by God with incredible potential. In a day of microchips and satellites, it is startling to remember that less than one hundred years ago men travelled by horse-drawn conveyances and existed without the benefits of telephones, computers, or FAX machines. Only a quarter of a century ago, those who predicted a day when many homes would have their own computers seemed to be dreaming.

But the potential God has given man is not limited to technological genius. Every man has possibilities beyond his present achievement in every area of life. He can do things with his body he has not yet attempted; he can discipline his mental capacities far beyond his present level of achievement; and he can develop his spiritual nature to be much more sensitive to the Spirit of God.

David contemplated the nature of man and wrote, "What is man, that thou art mindful of him? . . . For thou hast made him a little lower than the angels, and hast crowned him with glory and honour. Thou madest him to have dominion over the works of thy hands; thou hast put all things under his feet" (Psalm 8:4-6).

So man is made in the image of God, only a little lower than the angels, and he is crowned with glory and honor. God has made him to have dominion of all creation.

To determine how man can reach his full potential, it is necessary to briefly discuss anthropology, the doctrine of man. Any attempt to develop oneself without an understanding of the nature of man will fail.

Man, a Three-fold Being

God created man as body, soul, and spirit. The three-fold nature of man is seen in the Scriptures: "And the very God of peace sanctify you wholly; and I pray God your whole spirit and soul and body be preserved blameless unto the coming of our Lord Jesus Christ" (I Thessalonians 5:23).

"For the word of God is quick, and powerful, and sharper than any twoedged sword, piercing even to the dividing asunder of soul and spirit, and of the joints and marrow, and is a discerner of the thoughts and intents of the heart" (Hebrews 4:12).

What is the significance of each of the three parts of man's being?

The Body

We probably know more about the body than about the soul and spirit, for the body is the only visible part of man. It is the part of man that receives the most attention and care. Those who have no concern whatsoever for their spirit may be extremely interested in their body.

But the physical body—the flesh, bones, and blood—is merely a temporary dwelling for the soul and spirit. It daily grows older and closer to death. "Though our outward man [physical body] perish, yet the inward man [spirit] is renewed day by day" (II Corinthians 4:16).

Man will always have a body, but it will not be this present physical body which is uniquely adapted to the environment of this earth.

"For we know that if our earthly house of this tabernacle [physical body] were dissolved, we have a building of God, an house not made with hands, eternal in the heavens. For in this we groan, earnestly desiring to be clothed upon with our house which is from heaven: If so be that being clothed we shall not be found naked" (II Corinthians 5:1-3).

Paul compared the resurrection body with the present physical body using the analogy of seed and fruit, differing bodies given to various living things, and the varied brightness given to the stars of heaven.

"But some man will say, How are the dead raised up? and with what body do they come? Thou fool, that which thou sowest is not quickened, except it die: And that which thou sowest, thou sowest not that body that shall be, but bare grain, it may chance of wheat, or of some other grain: But God giveth it a body as it hath pleased him, and to every seed his own body. All flesh is not the same flesh. . . . There are also celestial bodies, and bodies terrestrial. . . . There is one glory of the sun, and another glory of the moon. . . . So also is the resurrection of the dead . . ." (I Corinthians 15:35-42).

The eternal, resurrection body is a spiritual body (I Corinthians 15:44). But while on this earth, man must cope with the present physical body.

The Soul

The soul is a part of the spirit man. Sometimes in the Scriptures the words *soul* and *spirit* are used as synonyms. At other times, however, there is a distinction which can be drawn between the two, and there are times when "soul" will not suffice; only "spirit" will do.

As far as we can determine, the soul of man has to do with his mind, will, and emotions. In other words, man's mental, volitional, and emotional nature resides in his soul.

The Spirit

The spirit of man seems to be the inner man, the real man who will live forever somewhere. This is man's essential nature.

The spirit seems to have senses which correspond to the physical senses.

"But strong meat belongeth to them that are of full age, even those who by reason of use have their senses exercised to discern both good and evil" (Hebrews 5:14). It is not by one's physical senses that good and evil are discerned, but by his spirit.

Spiritual senses are also indicated in the following Scriptures: "O taste and see that the LORD is good . . ." (Psalm 34:8). The physical taste buds are not involved here; this is a spiritual sense of taste.

"He that hath an ear, let him hear what the Spirit saith unto the churches . . ." (Revelation 2:11). This speaks not of the physical ear; all men have ears. Spiritual hearing is in view.

"While we look not at the things which are seen, but at the things which are not seen . . ." (II Corinthians 4:18). If the natural eye were the topic of discussion here, it would be a paradox to say that we should look at things which are not seen. The point is that there are some things not seen by the natural eye which are visible to the eye of the spirit.

"But I have all, and abound: I am full, having received of Epaphroditus the things which were sent from you, an odour of a sweet smell, a sacrifice acceptable, wellpleasing to God" (Philippians 4:18). The gift given to Paul was not a pleasant fragrance to his natural nostrils. It was a sweet smell in the realm of the spirit.

"Who being past feeling have given themselves over unto lasciviousness, to work all uncleanness with greediness" (Ephesians 4:19). These who are spiritually blinded have not lost their physical sense of feeling or touch. They have neglected their spiritual feeling so long and to such an extent that it is no longer sensitive.

It is by means of man's spirit that he is conscious of and communicates with God. By his spiritual senses, he can see, hear, smell, taste, and feel the spirit realm. This should be expected, since God Himself is a Spirit (John 4:24).

Keys to True Success

Any philosophy of success which ignores any part of man's being is doomed to failure. For a man to truly succeed and be all he can be, he must develop himself spiritually, mentally, and physically. How can this be done?

A man must be born again. The new birth affects man's being. Jesus said, "That which is born of the flesh is flesh; and that which is born of the Spirit is spirit" (John 3:6). The birth of the spirit is necessary because of sin. When Adam transgressed, he suffered spiritual death. In essence, spiritual death is separation from fellowship with God.

"And you hath he quickened, who were dead in trespasses and sins" (Ephesians 2:1).

"Verily, verily, I say unto you, He that heareth my word, and believeth on him that sent me, hath everlasting life, and shall not come into condemnation; but is passed from death unto life" (John 5:24).

"Wherefore, as by one man sin entered into the world, and death by sin; and so death passed upon all men, for that all have sinned" (Romans 5:12).

A man who is not born again has no fellowship with God. His mind is vain, his understanding darkened, and he is alienated from the life of God (Ephesians 4:17-18).

The first step a man must take in becoming all that God meant him to be is to be born again. Without this experience, there can be no true success.

A man must master his mind. The mind is a part of man's soul. In order for a man to succeed, his mind must be renewed by becoming under the control of the Spirit. "And be not conformed to this world: but be ye transformed by the renewing of your mind, that ye may prove what is that good, and acceptable, and perfect, will of God" (Romans 12:2).

The matter of conformity to the world has to do with a mind that is not renewed. As Proverbs 23:7 indicates, a man is what he thinks. The necessity of renewing one's mind is seen in the fact that human thoughts are vastly different from God's thoughts: "For my thoughts are not your thoughts, neither are your ways my ways, saith the LORD. For as the heavens are higher than the earth, so are my ways higher than your ways, and my thoughts than your thoughts" (Isaiah 55:8-9).

The most concise statement as to how to renew one's mind is found in Philippians 4:8. "Finally, brethren, whatsoever things are true, whatsoever things are honest, whatsoever things are just, whatsoever things are pure, whatsoever things are lovely, whatsoever things are of good report; if there be any virtue, and if there be any praise, think on these things."

This eight-fold test of every potential thought would eliminate negativism, skepticism, dishonesty, impurity, violence, and every other undesirable thought pattern.

An indispensable part of the renewing of the mind is meditation on the Word of God. Meditation is simply thinking deeply upon a subject. As a person thinks deeply on a specific verse of Scripture, turning it over and over in his mind, God will show him additional truths from His Word.

A Christian is admonished to bring every thought into captivity to Christ.

A man must conquer his will. The will is also a part of man's soul. In order to succeed, a man must overcome any tendency to be stubborn or rebellious. His will must be submitted to God's will.

A man's will can be the means that brings a person to higher achievement. His will should be the vehicle to discipline his actions from morning to night. It can be used to keep him from detrimental habits.

An international best-selling author, commenting on the rewards and responsibilities of success, wryly explained that one of the rewards of success is that no one can tell you what to do and make you go to work at nine o'clock in the morning. So, he said, he doesn't go to work at nine o'clock. He goes to work at six or seven in the morning. The point is obvious: Those who would succeed must go beyond what the ordinary person is willing to do. Most do the bare minimum in order to get by; those who will succeed use the force of their will to get up earlier and work harder than their peers.

A man must control his emotions. When a man is born again, he has the God-given ability to control his emotions rather than allowing his emotions to control him. "For God hath not given us the spirit of fear; but of power, and of love, and of a sound mind" (II Timothy 1:7).

The successful man will be emotionally stable. He will not be a stoic, void of emotions, but he will keep his emotions in check.

Although he may suffer depression or mental fatigue, the wise man will determine in advance not to make any major decisions under the duress of negative emotions. He realizes that, in most cases, emotional extremes will moderate with the passing of time. "Weeping may endure for a night, but joy cometh in the morning" (Psalm 30:5).

A man must discipline his body. While physical effort is of little spiritual value (I Timothy 4:8), a man should take reasonable care of his body. A body whose health has been neglected can be a negative drain on one's spiritual activities.

The man who would be all he can be will discipline his body to be a servant to the Holy Ghost. "I beseech you therefore, brethren, by the mercies of God, that ye present your bodies a living sacrifice, holy, acceptable unto God, which is your reasonable service" (Romans 12:1).

He will not permit sin to rule in his body. Instead he will yield his physical members as instruments of righteousness to God. (See Romans 6:12-13.)

Paul's Advice to Timothy

In I Timothy 6, Paul wrote about many things which contribute to success in life.

We will apply them to life in our day.
- Employees should honor their employers (verse 1).
- If a person has a Christian employer, he should be even more careful to honor him (verse 2).
- Gain must not be mistaken for godliness (verse 5).
- True success comes from a coupling of godliness and contentment (verse 6).
- A man should be content with food and clothing (verse 8).
- Those who have a goal of being rich bring to themselves many unnecessary temptations (verses 9-10).
- The Christian man should turn from the world's definition of success and set goals pertaining to righteousness, godliness, faith, love, patience, and meekness (verse 11).
- A man should never give up his faith (verse 12).
- Those who are rich should be generous in helping others (verses 17-19).
- A man should protect precious truths he has received (verse 20).
- A man should avoid worthless and empty talk and theories (verse 20).

Paul's advice should not be taken to mean that men should be complacent. There is a great difference between contentment and complacency. A man can be content with his present state—grateful for what God has done in his life up to that point—while still setting goals for the future.

And God has ordained that the man who aims high—setting for himself the highest standards for his personal behavior, performance, and morality—will surpass his greatest dreams.

Test Your Knowledge

1. Explain man's three-fold nature.
2. What are the five things a man must do to succeed?
3. List the eight qualifications Paul gave for appropriate thoughts.
4. How can a man avoid being conformed to the world?
5. What is the difference between contentment and complacency?

Apply Your Knowledge

Examine your present level of achievement in each of the following areas: (1) Are you born again? (2) Is your mind renewed? (3) Have you conquered your will? (4) Are you able to control your emotions? (5) Is your body a hindrance or a help in reaching your goals?

List three specific goals you hope to accomplish within the next year. Now list intermediate, monthly, and weekly steps you will take to be sure you reach them.

Memorize Philippians 4:8. Learn to subject each potential meditation to that checklist before you allow it to lodge in your mind.

Expand Your Knowledge

Learn to be more discerning about your three-fold nature. Recognize that, since you are body, soul, and spirit, impulses may come from each area. You should be able to distinguish between those impulses which come from the body (outer man) and those which come from the spirit (inner man).

Obtain and read the book by Daniel L. Segraves, *Insights for Christian Living* (Hazelwood, MO: Word Aflame Press, 1988).

Here I Stand

Wherefore take unto you the whole armour of God, that ye may be able to withstand in the evil day, and having done all, to stand.

Ephesians 6:13

Start With the Scriptures

II Chronicles 34:8-13
Ecclesiastes 9:10-11
Daniel 1:1-8, 17-21; 5:10-17; 6:4-23
Revelation 2:10

I Corinthians 16:13
Ephesians 6:14
Colossians 4:7-9
Hebrews 3:14

There are few qualities as appreciated as faithfulness. A person may be highly skilled and more talented than anyone else in his field of expertise, but if he is undependable his skill and talent quickly fade into insignificance. It has been said that availability is of greater importance than mere ability. In the same sense, ability is secondary to dependability.

Dependability is especially appreciated in men. Christian men should be leaders in their families, churches, and communities. A man's faithfulness to his commitments will be noticed by others and longer appreciated than his abilities.

In this chapter we will examine the need for steadfastness, faithfulness, and consistency. As Christian men lead their families steadfastly, exercising faithfulness and consistency before others, they exemplify the Lord Jesus Christ.

Here I Stand

"A man ought to be a man!" How many times have we heard the statement? A person may make that statement appealing for masculine attire or actions in contrast to effeminacy. Equally important and also implied by the words, however, is the fact that a man should fill his God-given role of leadership within the family. (See chapter one.)

A man is to lead his family, friends, and associates by example and by instruction. While he is not to be overbearing, he is nonetheless to lead with strength and conviction. He should not fear asserting his position with love, kindness, clarity, and consistency. These traits are indications of a good leader.

Steadfastly serving God is perhaps the strongest exercise of human leadership that a man can offer his family and others. When a man is steadfast in his faith, ideals, and convictions, those who follow him will have confidence in his leadership. When he vacillates in his commitment to God, however, the confidence of others in his ability to lead is shaken.

The Steadfastness of Daniel

One of the great biblical examples of steadfastness is the life of Daniel. Even Daniel's name seems to indicate his deep commitment to God: "God is my judge."

It is apparent that Daniel's purpose in life was anchored to one commitment—to serve God faithfully. Although captive in the strange and idolatrous land of Babylon, Daniel purposed in his heart that he would not defile himself (Daniel 1:8).

Daniel was only a young man when he was taken into Babylon. His three companions, Hananiah, Mishael, and Azariah (unfortunately known better by their pagan, Babylonian names: Shadrach, Meshach, and Abednego), were probably about the same age as Daniel. All these young men evidently developed some tremendous qualities of steadfastness and devotion to God. They consistently refused to compromise their principles even though they had many opportunities.

Many Babylonian young men had the same natural qualities as Daniel and his three Hebrew friends, but the king chose them because of their distinction from all the others. God had blessed Daniel, Hananiah, Mishael, and Azariah in a special way because of their commitment and steadfastness to Him, and as a result they rose above all of their peers in the king's eyes. (See Daniel 1:8-21.)

Sometimes as Pentecostals we feel distinct and different from others in the world. The truth is that we *are* different! As our God-given talents and qualities are recognized by others, we often receive special respect. Our steadfastness in our commitment to Jesus Christ will not detract from our talents and abilities; rather it will amplify them.

Steadfast in Purpose

Daniel and the other Hebrews possessed a steadfastness of purpose (Daniel 1:8). Daniel purposed in his heart not to defile himself by eating the king's meat or by drinking his wine. Apparently Hananiah, Mishael, and Azariah joined in Daniel's commitment.

After eating only vegetables for ten days, they were examined and compared to the Babylonians who had been eating meat. (See Daniel 1:8-15.) They were fairer and fleshier than all of those who had consumed a regular diet.

Their decision of abstinence was an effort to keep themselves pure from the idolatry of the Babylonians. In Babylon, the Hebrew God was not recognized; rather He was mocked. The meat that the Babylonians ate was significant to their idolatrous worship. Realizing this, Daniel and his friends refused the meat and drink of the Babylonians in order to glorify the true God.

The devotion of the Hebrews was motivated by their intense steadfastness of purpose. They had been taught to recognize right from wrong. They could have violated their convictions and excused themselves as captives in a foreign land. Rather they took their stand with steadfastness in the face of ridicule and abuse, and they glorified God.

Men need a basic sense of purpose and steadfastness to God and right principles. There are many opportunities to compromise our basic knowledge of right and wrong—at work, in business dealings, or with certain friends. When such temptations confront us, only our faithfulness to a deep sense of purpose and resolve can keep us true to God.

Every person needs a cause to which he dedicates his entire life. Everything in that person's life then becomes secondary to the cause to which his life has been devoted. There is no greater cause to which a Christian man can devote himself than to that of living a committed Christian life.

Steadfast in Unity

These Hebrew men possessed a steadfastness of unity with one another (Daniel 2:17-18). Their unity was apparent in the second year of King Nebuchadnezzar's reign. The king was troubled by his dreams. When he could not sleep, the king called for the magicians, astrologers, and sorcerers—all of Babylon's wise men—to interpret his dreams. None of the king's wise men were able to provide an interpretation. Infuriated, the king decreed to destroy all of Babylon's wise men.

When the king's men came to slay Daniel and the Hebrews, Daniel sought an audience with the king to request time to seek an interpretation. The king granted his request.

Daniel immediately went to his companions and revealed the situation. The four of them agreed to seek God's mercy and an interpretation.

Daniel recognized the strength of unity, and so should Christian men today. We can accomplish much more together than any one of us can do alone. There is strength and power in a unified agreement. Jesus said, "If two of you shall agree on earth as touching any thing that they shall ask, it shall be done for them of my Father which is in heaven" (Matthew 18:19).

Jesus said that a divided house, one without unity, cannot stand. Unity is the cohesive element that binds individuals together within a common purpose. Only as the church is unified can it really progress and move forward in God's plan.

Steadfast in Worship

Worship is a powerful force in this world. According to one definition, *worship* is "unbounded admiration; intense love; extreme devotion" *(Webster's New Universal Unabridged Dictionary).*

Whether a person wishes to admit it or not, he will worship something. In modern society, reverent homage is paid to many inanimate objects. Perhaps a person may not think that he is "worshiping" or "idolizing" an object or activity of life, but if he is giving it supreme devotion and priority in his life, then he is worshiping it. Some people worship cars, houses, land, clothes, or other materialistic goals. Other people give various activities such as sports events or even their jobs top priority in their lives. Apostle Paul referred to this as creature worship.

"Who changed the truth of God into a lie, and worshipped and served the creature more than the Creator, who is blessed for ever. Amen" (Romans 1:25).

Paul also spoke of the perilous "last days" in his second letter to Timothy. (See II Timothy 3:1-5.) It seems that the impetus for creature worship is an intense love for pleasure which surpasses one's love for God. Men begin to subtly worship themselves, creating an extremely self-centered society.

Even in the midst of a self-centered society, Christian men can be leaders in true worship. We can begin by having a supreme devotion to God. Further, we can live exemplary, balanced lives where nothing supersedes the value and importance of God.

Daniel was steadfast in his worship of God (Daniel 2:19-23). Daniel did not feel smug or confident in himself when he received the secret of the dream. Rather, he began to worship and glorify God. He quickly acknowledged that all wisdom, might, and knowledge belong to God.

God moves through the channel of worship. The more we worship Him, the more He is able to do for us. As we acknowledge Him in our lives, He directs our paths (Proverbs 3:5-7). Through worship we can defeat our problems by gaining God's assistance.

Not only did Daniel persevere in his worship of God, he steadfastly exhibited a spirit of selflessness (Daniel 2:47-49). Daniel revealed the interpretation of the dream to Nebuchadnezzar and gave all the credit and glory to God.

Nebuchadnezzar honored Daniel, gave him many gifts and made him ruler over the whole province of Babylon. Daniel, however, could not accept such honor and forget his friends who had sought God with him for the answer. He remembered Hananiah, Mishael, and Azariah and requested a place of leadership for them. How easy it would have been for Daniel to forget them in his moment of glory and honor! But his deep sense of character would not permit him to overlook their sacrifice and assistance.

It is easy for us to seek the help of our peers when we are in trouble but forget them when things are going well. True friends are faithful in good times and bad times alike. A real friend loves at all times (Proverbs 17:17).

Steadfast in Prayer

In an age when the temporal pleasures of the world have been placed in prominence, God needs men who know how to prevail in prayer. Prayer is the lifeline of the Christian, but it is also the pathway of spiritual accomplishment. In other words, a Christian must pray to maintain his spiritual relationship with Jesus Christ. But if that Christian desires to accomplish spiritual goals and achievements, prayer alone is not sufficient. He must steadfastly *prevail* in prayer.

Men should be leaders of prayer within their homes and communities. Wives and children usually wait for their husband or father to call the family to prayer. It is easy for Christians to become overly busy and allow less important matters to steal from them their passion for prayer. It is the man's responsibility to remind his family, "It's time to pray."

Daniel was steadfast in prayer (Daniel 6:10). Jealousy among certain Babylonians prompted them to design a plot against Daniel. They persuaded King

Darius to sign a decree calling for the cessation of all petitions of any God or man for thirty days. Once the plot was set in order, the jealous men waited for Daniel to break the order, which they knew he would do. They had confidence in Daniel's consistent prayer life.

Daniel did not have to decide that he would violate the decree; there was no decision to make. He simply continued to pray as he always did—three times each day. He was consistent in prayer, and no decree could change that.

After Daniel was found guilty of violating the decree, he was thrown to the lions for one night. King Darius spent that sleepless night worried about his friend Daniel. Early the next morning the king discovered that Daniel had been unharmed by the lions. Because Daniel had been steadfast in the face of opposition, God was faithful to him and shut the mouths of the lions.

God will honor and bless those who are consistent in prayer. Prayer becomes the great shield of God's protection and providence over our life.

Prayer not only helps us overcome problems, but it builds and maintains a person's relationship with Jesus Christ. A person's relationship with Christ then gives him confidence that whatever happens in life, God's presence and protection is with him.

Steadfast unto Death

Hananiah, Mishael, and Azariah were steadfast in the face of imminent death (Daniel 3:16-18). Nebuchadnezzar made a golden image and called all the rulers of Babylon to its dedication. At this dedication a decree was issued that at the sound of the music every person must fall down and worship the golden image. "And whoso falleth not down and worshippeth shall the same hour be cast into the midst of a burning fiery furnace" (Daniel 3:6).

The three Hebrews refused to bow down and worship the image. As they were called before Nebuchadnezzar to give an account of their actions, they boldly answered him. "We are not careful to answer thee in this matter. If it be so, our God whom we serve is able to deliver us. . . . But if not, be it known unto thee, O king, that we will not serve thy gods, nor worship the golden image which thou hast set up" (Daniel 3:16-18).

They were faithful and courageous in the face of certain death. They were determined to do what was right even if it cost them their lives. What faith and courage prompted them to say, "He is able to deliver us, but whether He does or not, we will not bow!"

The true test of steadfastness is its long-term endurance. Steadfastness cannot accurately be measured by a person's response to one situation. It is recognizable only as the result of a lifetime commitment that is faithfully executed throughout the years of the person's life.

Faithfulness—A Way of Life

Faithfulness is not just something a person does; it is a way of life. When a person is faithful to God, circumstances and environment do not affect or change his commitment to Christian principles. Christianity is not like a job, from which a person might take a two-week vacation once a year. It is a chosen lifestyle of following godly principles to which a person makes a lifetime commitment.

Christians are stewards of God, and as such, we are required to be faithful. (See I Corinthians 4:2.) We should not have to decide whether or not to be faithful to God. Like Daniel, we should simply act on the basis of our commitment to God.

Consistency—A Jewel

Some people are as fickle and changeable as the weather. They are governed by emotion and feeling instead of knowledge. Their lives, like a listing ship out of control, have no impetus, no definite direction. They do not really know what they want to achieve in life, or how to reach for specific goals. They live unhappy lives and endure a spectrum of emotional lows. They live in constant change.

Biblical principles never change. God's Word is unchanging, solid, and consistent in a world that is continually changing. "The grass withereth, the flower fadeth: but the word of our God shall stand forever" (Isaiah 40:8).

God is Himself constant in nature. "For I am the LORD, I change not" (Malachi 3:6). The Book of Hebrews records, "Jesus Christ the same yesterday, and to day, and for ever" (Hebrews 13:8).

The Lord also desires for His people to be consistent and steadfast. He wishes for them to faithfully execute their Christian duties and abide in the faith. Apostle Paul wrote to the Corinthian church, "Therefore, my beloved brethren, be ye stedfast, unmoveable, always abounding in the work of the Lord" (I Corinthians 15:58). (See also II Thessalonians 2:15.)

Instability within a man is practically intolerable. The Lord vehemently condemned the man who is unfaithful in providing for his family (I Timothy 5:8). We readily think this refers to financial care; however, there are many other obligations by which a man cares for his family. Obviously, a primary responsibility of a man is the constant, steadfast leading of his family in spiritual matters.

It is often easier for a man to avoid confrontation than to take a stand for God. Elizabeth Clarke Dunn once said, "Change is an easy panacea. It takes character to stay in one place and be happy there."

It is the Christian man's duty to do his best to prepare for every circumstance of opposition which he may face in life. And when he has done all that he can do, God asks only that he "stand" (Ephesians 6:13-14).

Test Your Knowledge

True or False

_____ 1. Ability is more important than dependability.

_____ 2. Man's role within the family structure as ordained by God is a subservient role.

_____ 3. It is unacceptable for a man to be an overbearing ruler as his family leader.

_____ 4. If a man fails God, it has little effect upon those who follow his leadership.

_____ 5. Daniel's one purpose in life was to serve God faithfully.

_____ 6. Daniel's refusal to eat the king's meat was a decision of inconsequence.

_____ 7. Every man needs a basic sense of purpose for his life.

_____ 8. Alone, Daniel selfishly relished his new role as a ruler of Babylon.

_____ 9. Modern society is basically self-centered.

_____ 10. God is dependable, but He does not desire us to exhibit that characteristic.

Apply Your Knowledge

How dependable are you? Are you always late for appointments or for church? Do you keep your commitments to others? Is there room for improvement?

Use the following list to evaluate your dependability and to chart a plan for improvement.

Item	Consistent?			
	Always	Usually	Sometimes	Never
Church Attendance..........				
On Time for Church.........				
Help on Church Workdays ...				
Finish Projects				
Have Private Devotions......				
Lead Family Devotions				
Give Best in Worship........				
Get Along with Others.......				

Expand Your Knowledge

For further study of this subject, consider the two books: *100%* by Fred Hartley and *Call to Discipleship* by Juan Carlos Ortiz.

The Golden Rule 12

Therefore all things whatsoever ye would that men should do to you, do ye even so to them: for this is the law and the prophets.

Matthew 7:12

Start With the Scriptures

Matthew 5:1-16;
22:37-40

Romans 12:13-21
I John 3:18

Never one to waste words, Jesus had a way of reducing great truths to their most succinct, precise form. An example of this, concerning human relationships, occurs in Matthew 7:12: "Therefore all things whatsoever ye would that men should do to you, do ye even so to them: for this is the law and the prophets."

The wisdom of this truth is so universally recognized, even among those who may know very little about any other portion of Scripture, that it is widely known as "The Golden Rule."

Many businesses attribute their success to their adherence to the Golden Rule. Some have even adopted the words as a motto expressing corporate philosophy. The rule is simple, yet profound: Treat others the way you would want them to treat you.

While volumes have been written and many seminars conducted on the subject of interpersonal relationships, the wisdom of the Golden Rule cannot be improved upon.

The Wisdom of the Old Testament

When Jesus gave this statement concerning the treatment of others, He added, "for this is the law and the prophets." A similar phrase is found in Matthew 22:37-40. "Jesus said unto him, Thou shalt love the Lord thy God with all thy heart, and with all thy soul, and with all thy mind. This is the first and great commandment. And the second is like unto it, Thou shalt love thy neighbour as thyself. On these two commandments hang all the law and the prophets."

The point of this is that all the teachings of the Old Testament can be summed up in these two truths:
- Love God;
- Love others.

The word *hang* in the statement "on these two commandments hang all the law and the prophets" is used to describe the way a cloak hangs on a peg driven into the wall. In other words, the entire Old Testament is supported by these two commandments. Without them, the Old Testament would collapse.

Concerning one's relationship with God, the essence of the Old Testament is: Love God with all your heart, soul, mind, and strength. Concerning one's relationship with others, the essence of the Old

Testament is: Love others as yourself.

The Golden Rule is another way of saying the essence of the Old Testament command to love God and our neighbor. It emphasizes the practical aspects of love. Love is not demonstrated by the way one *feels;* it is demonstrated by what one *does.*

The Wisdom of the New Testament

While Christianity is God-centered, as opposed to humanistic, people-centered religions, it has a great deal to say about human relationships. A large portion of the epistles addresses this subject. (See the list of Scriptures in Expand Your Knowledge.)

The reason for this emphasis on man's relationship with man is that God made man in His own image. To a certain degree, therefore, anything done to a person is done to the Lord Himself.

This is seen in the Bible as early as Genesis 9:6, where God instituted capital punishment based on the fact that an attack on man is an attack on the image of God.

It is also seen as late as James 3:9-10 where verbal abuse of a person is also condemned on the basis of man being in the image (similitude) of God.

The Proof of Love

While the romanticized Hollywood version of love emphasizes feelings, the Scriptures demand that love be proved by actions. "Wherefore shew ye to them, and before the churches, the proof of your love, and of our boasting on your behalf" (II Corinthians 8:24). In this case, the proof of love that Paul expected was for the church at Corinth to give to assist others in need.

John also addressed the matter of translating professed love into action: "My little children, let us not love in word, neither in tongue; but in deed and in truth" (I John 3:18).

This expression, reminiscent of the influence of the Hebrew language, does not mean that John did not want Christians to express their love verbally but that he did not want it to end there. In other words, they were not to love in word or in tongue *only* but also in deed and in truth.

A Christian man demonstrates his love for others by use of the Golden Rule.

The Golden Rule at Work

In Romans 12:13-21, Paul listed practical steps in the treatment of both friends and enemies. First, we will consider what he had to say about the treatment of friends. Then we will consider what he instructs us in our treatment of enemies.

The Treatment of Friends

"Distributing to the necessity of saints . . ." (verse 13). The Christian should stand ready to give whatever is necessary to help his brothers and sisters in need. This is what he would want them to do if he were the one in need.

James was precise on this point. "If a brother or sister be naked, and destitute of daily food, and one of you say unto them, Depart in peace, be ye warmed and filled; notwithstanding ye give them not those things which are needful to the body; what doth it profit?" (James 2:15-16).

Here is an example of love in word only: a Christian is in need of clothing or food. Another expresses his concern and love only in what he says. He does nothing to help in a practical way.

There is no profit to love that extends only to verbal confessions of concern. If a brother is in need of clothing, love is demonstrated in providing clothing to him. If he is in need of food, providing food demonstrates love.

This practical demonstration of love should begin among brethren, though it will extend beyond that. Paul wrote, "As we have therefore opportunity, let us do good unto all men, especially unto them who are of the household of faith" (Galatians 6:10). This is the counterpart of Jesus' statement concerning the proof of discipleship. "By this shall all men know that ye are my disciples, if ye have love one to another" (John 13:35).

"... *Given to hospitality* ..." *(verse 13)*. The word *hospitality* is translated from a Greek word which literally has to do with loving strangers. In this case, the love is expressed by the opening of one's home in a time of need.

In some nations of the world hospitality of sharing the home has become almost a lost art, especially with the advent of hotels and motels. Of course, it is often more desirable, especially to ministers and their families who travel constantly, to lodge in hotels and motels for the sake of privacy.

But in the early church, the lodging in homes of brothers and sisters in need, and especially of traveling ministers, was a well-known demonstration of Christian love. It was so characteristic of Christians that it was noted even by unbelievers. As time went by, larger churches or those on important trade routes established hospices for travelers.

While it is not necessary to attempt to force the culture of the early Christians in the Roman world on every nation and people, it is important to fulfill the underlying purpose of the command. That is, in every situation where a genuine need for hospitality exists, the Christian should be willing to do whatever is necessary to minister to the needs of others.

"Rejoice with them that do rejoice, and weep with them that weep" (verse 15). The Golden Rule does not end with sympathy. It extends to empathy: identification with another. When one's friends are happy and joyous, one should share their joy. In the time of a tragic event, one should also share their grief.

Some people mistakenly think that the best way to deal with their friends' grief is to attempt to "cheer them up." But Solomon shared Paul's insight. He said, "As he that taketh away a garment in cold weather, and as vinegar upon nitre, so is he that singeth songs to an heavy heart" (Proverbs 25:20). All three situations include inappropriate acts. Cold weather is a time for warm garments. When vinegar is added to nitre (similar to a carbonated soda water), both lose their usefulness. And a person with a heavy heart does not need to hear songs; he needs someone to share his sorrow.

Some well-meaning people think the proper response to those who are joyous is to remind them of the possibility of coming calamity. Some seem convinced that a string of positive events guarantees impending tragedy.

But the mystery of knowing what to say to another, whether he is rejoicing or grieving, is answered by this simple counsel: identify with a friend in his joys and sorrows.

"Be of the same mind one toward another. Mind not high things, but condescend to men of low estate. Be not wise in your own conceits" (verse 16). The first sentence of this verse seems to conclude the point of the previous verse: look at situations from the other person's point of view. Then Paul encouraged the Romans not to limit their personal concern to those of high esteem in society. They were, instead, to show equal care for those with no social standing.

Human wisdom would suggest that there could be no profit in helping the poor, but that if one demonstrated concern about those who were rich, he would gain favor with them.

Just the opposite is true. Solomon declared, "He that oppresseth the poor to increase his riches, and he that giveth to the rich, shall surely come to want" (Proverbs 22:16). On the other hand, "He that hath pity upon the poor lendeth unto the LORD; and that which he hath given will he pay him again" (Proverbs 19:17).

The Lord is so personally concerned with the practice of the Golden Rule, and particularly with our treatment of the poor, that He considers help to the poor as a personal gift, and He will reward the person who practices this kind of charity.

The last advice Paul gave in Romans 12:16 is, *"Be not wise in your own conceits."* That is, forsake your own wisdom. Often, the thing that seems right is precisely the wrong thing to do.

Isaiah said, "For my thoughts are not your thoughts, neither are your ways my ways, saith the LORD. For as the heavens are higher than the earth, so are my ways higher than your ways, and my thoughts than your thoughts" (Isaiah 55:8-9).

The Treatment of Enemies

In Romans 12, Paul also addressed the proper treatment of one's enemies.

"Bless them which persecute you: bless, and curse not" (verse 14). This is reminiscent of Jesus' counsel in the Sermon on the Mount. "Ye have heard that it hath been said, Thou shalt love thy neighbour, and hate thine enemy. But I say unto you, Love your enemies, bless them that curse you, do good to them that hate you, and pray for them which despitefully use you, and persecute you; That ye may be the children of your Father which is in heaven: for he maketh his sun to rise on the evil and on the good,

and sendeth rain on the just and on the unjust" (Matthew 5:43-45).

Underlying this counsel is the aim of thinking and acting as God does toward those who reject Him. Since God is God, He could instantly pulverize all who reject Him. Instead, He bears with them, continuing to bless them even in their rejection of Him, hoping they will come to repentance.

This is seen in that He causes the sun to shine and the rain to fall on both those who surrender to Him and those who reject Him. Some have thought the sun to be a symbol of blessing and the rain a symbol of problems and difficulties in this passage. Thus they interpret it to mean that God allows both good things and bad things to happen to all, regardless of their relationship with Him.

Instead, both the sun and the rain are symbols of blessing. Either alone would be disaster. Paul said, "Nevertheless he left not himself without witness, in that he did good, and gave us rain from heaven, and fruitful seasons, filling our hearts with food and gladness" (Acts 14:17). The rain from heaven is a witness of God's goodness.

Jesus' advice in the Sermon on the Mount went beyond merely saying, "Love your enemies." Had He ended there, some could possibly have claimed love while rejecting the enemy.

Jesus gave three specific actions to take to demonstrate love: ❶ Bless them that curse you; ❷ Do good to them that hate you; and ❸ Pray for them which despitefully use you.

All of these are outworkings of the Golden Rule. And if there is any possibility of restoration to fellowship with an enemy, it will come as a result of this radical action.

"Recompense to no man evil for evil. Provide things honest in the sight of all men" (verse 17). When an individual repays evil with evil, he perpetuates

a chain of negative events which may have no ending. But when he renders good for evil, he breaks the chain, demonstrates his sincerity (honesty), and may actually bring about the healing of the broken relationship.

It is absolutely imperative, of course, that all of this be done without any hint of a pious, "holier-than-thou" or "suffering martyr" complex. Indeed, before a person even begins his attempt to do good for an enemy, it would probably be best to exercise the other portion of the Lord's counsel: to pray for one's enemy. The prayer should contain a sincere request for God to bless one's enemy. This will help an individual purify his motives. Then he can approach the other aspects of his relationship with his enemy with transparent honesty.

"If it be possible, as much as lieth in you, live peaceably with all men" (verse 18). Simply put, a Christian man must apply all his ability and will to living in peace with others. The statement "as much as lieth in you" implies that effort will be required, since it is easier to be at peace with some than with others.

But nothing short of a total commitment is acceptable. While in the final analysis it may be impossible to live at peace with some, this must never be due to a lack of effort on the part of the Christian.

"Dearly beloved, avenge not yourselves, but rather give place unto wrath: for it is written, Vengeance is mine; I will repay, saith the Lord" (verse 19). Any attempt to "get even" with another is an effort to play God. Vengeance is God's territory, and no human being is suited to properly dispense it. When an individual has been wronged, he should accept that wrong in a spirit of meekness, while trusting God to make it right.

"Whoso diggeth a pit shall fall therein: and he that rolleth a stone, it will return upon him" (Proverbs

26:27). The person who attempts to get vengeance will find his efforts coming home to him. Instead, a person should follow the example of Jesus, even when he has been wronged.

"Therefore if thine enemy hunger, feed him; if he thirst, give him drink: for in so doing thou shalt heap coals of fire on his head" (verse 20). In this statement, Paul is referring to Proverbs 25:21-22. The verse indicates that demonstrating practical love for one's enemy will have a desirable effect. It will "heap coals of fire on his head." This has been subject to several interpretations, but in the final analysis it seems certain that the point is this: Giving practical help to one's enemy (not just empty verbiage) when he is in need will result, if possible, in reconciliation. This is indeed borne out in the next verse.

"Be not overcome of evil, but overcome evil with good" (verse 21). The good news about the Golden Rule is that good is, after all, more powerful than evil. And when a person does good to those around him, he sets in motion a powerful force which will heal broken relationships, restore wounded spirits, and result in good things returning to him.

Summary

The person who practices the Golden Rule sets out with the planned intent of doing good to others. He will be alert to the needs of others, including the very real need to be recognized and commended for their efforts.

He will be kind and gentle, with the fruit of the Spirit growing profusely in his life. His interest in others will not be superficial, but sincere. He will not be a loner; he will love people and show them every needed hospitality.

The practice of the Golden Rule is not complicated. Whether a person is dealing with his wife, his children, his relatives, his neighbors, or his coworkers, he will simply ask himself: *How would I want to be treated in this situation?*

Without exception, to treat others the way one would want to be treated is the Christian thing to do. And in most cases, a commitment to this philosophy will minimize enmity and open up a broad world of love and friendship.

Test Your Knowledge

1. What verse of Scripture is the basis for the Golden Rule?
2. All of the teachings of the Old Testament can be summed up in what two truths?
3. Love is not demonstrated by the way one _____; it is demonstrated by what one _____.
4. According to John 13:35, how shall men know that we are Christ's disciples?
5. Define *sympathy* and *empathy*.
6. In the Sermon on the Mount, Jesus gave three specific actions to take to demonstrate love. List them.
7. When an individual repays evil with evil, he perpetuates a chain of negative events. What can this individual do to break this chain?
8. Should a Christian put forth any effort at living peaceably with all men?
9. To whom does vengeance belong?
10. What is the good news about the Golden Rule?

Apply Your Knowledge

Take some time alone to sit down and review your relationships during this past week. Did you always treat your wife the way you would want her to treat you? Do you expect something of her you are unwilling to give? If you were the child and your child was the father, would you be happy with the way you were treated? If another person went to your co-workers and asked them if you practice the Golden Rule, what would they say?

Look ahead to this next week. How can you demonstrate the Golden Rule? What can you do to treat your wife in a more loving way? How can you prove to your children your desire to be a more loving and compassionate father? What fellow worker do you need to take special care to minister to in a practical way?

Expand Your Knowledge

Included with this lesson is a lengthy list of references from the epistles dealing with human relationships. For the next six weeks, read portions of this list as a daily devotional. As you read, ask God to show you how you can apply the Scriptures to your life.

See, for example, Romans 12:13-21; 13; 14; 15:1-7; I Corinthians 1:10-11; 6:1-8; 8; 11:17-34; 13; II Corinthians 7:2; 8:7-24; 9; Galatians 6:2-10; Ephesians 4; 5:21-33; 6:1-9; Philippians 2:1-4; Colossians 3:8-9, 12-23; 4:1, 5-6; I Thessalonians 2:10-11; 3:12; 4:6-12; 5:12-15; II Thessalonians 3:11-15; I Timothy 3:1-13; 5:1-20; 6:1-5, 11, 17-19; II Timothy 2:24-25; Titus 1:6-16; 2:1-10; 3:1-3; Philemon; Hebrews 12:14; 13:1-7, 16-17, 24; James 1:26-27; 2:1-13; 3; 4:1-12; 5:1-9, 16, 19-20; I Peter 1:22; 2:1, 11-21; 3:1-11; 4:8-10, 15; 5:5, 14; I John 2:9-11; 3:14-18; 4:7-11, 20-21; 5:2, 16; II John 5; III John 5-8; Jude 16, 22-23.

Bloom Where You Are Planted 13

Let every man abide in the same calling wherein he was called.

I Corinthians 7:20

Start With the Scriptures

John 21:18-22
I Corinthians 7:17-24;
12:8-11

Ephesians 2:21-22

Although each man is made in the image of God, every one is an individual. It pleased God to make each person unique, with his own unduplicated combination of interests and abilities. Out of the more than five billion people on planet earth, no two are exactly alike.

Beyond the mere individualization of creation, Christianity is a personalized experience. When a man is born again, he is given a unique blend of gifts by the grace of God. Some of these are described in Romans 12:4-8 and I Corinthians 12:8-11.

While there is a framework within which all must fit, an ideal toward which each person reaches (Ephesians 4:13), there is considerable diversity within that framework. Indeed, the church is compared to the human body composed of many diverse members (I Corinthians 12:12-30; Romans 12:4) and to a physical building made up of living stones (Ephesians 2:21-22; I Peter 2:5).

In Ephesians 2:21, the building is described as being "fitly framed together." These words are translated from the Greek word *harmos,* which means "joint." According to J. A. Robinson in his book *St. Paul's Epistle to the Ephesians,* this word was used in ancient Greece in describing the process of building large structures. It referred to preparing the surfaces by cutting, rubbing, and testing, and to the preparation of the dowels and dowel holes, and to the fixing of the dowels with molten lead.

The church is not a temple formed by the random piling of rocks. It is fashioned from living stones, custom made for their precise location. Just as Solomon's Temple of old was built by stones hewed and shaped carefully in the stone quarries so that there was no sound of a hammer on the building site, so the church is composed of living stones carefully prepared by God for their precise function in the church.

The grace of God gives us the desire and power to do exactly His will (Philippians 2:13). But the enemy works to make us discontent and to believe that the grass on the other side of the fence is greener. If he can cause us to step away from the purpose for which God made us, he effectively destroys the potential we have in the kingdom of God (John 10:10). Paul addressed this problem in I Corinthians 7:17-24.

"But as God hath distributed to every man, as the

Lord hath called every one, so let him walk. And so ordain I in all churches. Is any man called being circumcised? let him not become uncircumcised. Is any called in uncircumcision? let him not be circumcised. . . . Let every man abide in the same calling wherein he was called. Art thou called being a servant? care not for it: but if thou mayest be made free, use it rather. . . . Brethren, let every man, wherein he is called, therein abide with God."

Perhaps we could sum up the intent of this passage in this way:
- You are where you are for a reason.
- Unless God opens the door for you to step through, stay where you are.
- Look around you for the opportunities within your grasp.

One of the principles by which God operates is that He expects us to take full advantage of every opportunity He gives us. As we do this, He will open to us more doors of opportunity. But if we fail to explore all the opportunities He presents, He will close doors which He would otherwise have opened.

This is illustrated in the parable of the talents (Matthew 25:14-30). In the parable, the master gave his servants differing amounts of talents according to their ability to use them. This illustrates individuality. It also points out that no one has been burdened with more opportunities than he can fulfill.

The two servants who used their talents and multiplied them received commendation upon the master's return. The one servant who, in fear, did not fulfill his potential was rebuked, and his talent was taken away to be given to one who had demonstrated his willingness to use what was given to him.

It has been said that success in life is not measured by what you are and what you have done, but by what you are and what you have done compared to what you could have been and could have done.

It is not wise to compare ourselves with others (II Corinthians 10:12), but we should reach for our highest potential. Like a flower carefully and lovingly planted by a master gardener, we should not fret that we were not planted elsewhere, but we should bloom where we are planted.

What Is That to You?

One of the most dramatic events of the last few days Jesus spent on earth is recorded in John 21:18-22. "Verily, verily, I say unto thee, When thou wast young, thou girdedst thyself, and walkedst whither thou wouldest: but when thou shalt be old, thou shalt stretch forth thy hands, and another shall gird thee, and carry thee whither thou wouldest not. This spake he, signifying by what death he should glorify God. And when he had spoken this, he saith unto him, Follow me. Then Peter, turning about, seeth the disciple whom Jesus loved following; which also leaned on his breast at supper, and said, Lord, which is he that betrayeth thee? Peter seeing him saith to Jesus, Lord, and what shall this man do? Jesus saith unto him, If I will that he tarry till I come, what is that to thee? follow thou me."

What Shall This Man Do?

This question reveals a lack of understanding shared with Peter by many. It is the idea that God must be "fair" according to man's perception, that He must treat everyone exactly alike. But God does not treat everyone alike. The reason is that no two people *are* alike.

God treats each person with *justice*. That is, He does exactly what is right with each individual.

Many puzzling questions are answered with the wisdom of Abraham. "Shall not the Judge of all the earth do right?" (Genesis 18:25).

In every situation, regardless of the circumstances, God's judgment will be that which is right. In the final analysis, no one will be able to accuse Him of prejudice or injustice.

The problem is that humans know so little. There is so much we do not see. We do not know the future. We make judgments based on our limited knowledge, but if we had more information we would change our decisions.

Peter's plaintive question is understandable. After all, if he was destined to martyrdom, should not John—and everybody else—suffer the same fate?

Jesus' response was apparently shocking. "If it is my wish that John live until I return, what business is that of yours? You follow me. Do not worry about others."

This poignant encounter dramatically reveals the master plan of God. He has a specific purpose involving precise placement and timing for each individual. It is the responsibility of the believer to fulfill that purpose, blooming where he is planted, without railing against God for planting others elsewhere and in differing circumstances.

How to Bloom Where You Are Planted

Do your best where you are. Solomon said, "Whatsoever thy hand findeth to do, do it with thy might; for there is no work, nor device, nor knowledge, nor wisdom, in the grave, whither thou goest" (Ecclesiastes 9:10).

Contrary to popular opinion, the grass on the other side of the fence is no greener. And even if it were, the grass on this side would become greener with the proper care and effort.

In his classic lecture, "Acres of Diamonds," minister Russell H. Conwell told the story of a man who sold his land to go on a worldwide search for diamonds. He died in a distant port, separated from his family and friends, penniless. Meanwhile, the purchaser of his property found it to be virtually awash in diamonds.

This story, and others like it, was designed to show people the neglected opportunities and possibilities immediately around them.

Those who obey the counsel of the Scriptures need never fear failure. The phrase "whatsoever thy hand findeth to do" implies diligence in meeting the needs always within one's view, if he will only open his eyes. Many who are quite sure they could rise to meet some great unidentified and unseen challenge will never have the opportunity, for they have failed to measure up to the smaller tasks God has given them.

The wisdom of God is quite different from the wisdom of man. The humanistic ideal of Marx was to take from those who have and give to those who have not. This redistribution of the wealth was supposed to create a society where all would be equal. It would be "from each according to his ability, to each according to his need."

Every attempt to enforce this philosophy has been a miserable failure. The reason is that God says, "For unto every one that hath shall be given, and he shall have abundance: but from him that hath not shall be taken away even that which he hath" (Matthew 25:29).

Can this be reasonable? Can it be just?

The unprofitable servant was wicked and slothful (Matthew 25:26). This was evidenced by his unwillingness to make use of the investment with which he was trusted. It would not have made any difference if he had received one talent, two, five, or a hundred. His response would have been the same: inactivity.

It is not that he did not have ability. The master had specifically given each man opportunity in direct proportion to his ability (Matthew 25:15). The problem was that the wicked servant refused to use his capabilities to fulfill his master's will.

God has made an investment in each person. And He wants each one to use that investment to the fullest extent.

No one knows where his use of God's investment will ultimately lead. But as the Lord observes faithfulness and excellence in the use of His gifts, He opens more doors of opportunity.

When they heard John the Baptist, the common people, publicans, and soldiers asked, "What shall we do then?" (Luke 3:10). John answered, "He that hath two coats, let him impart to him that hath none; and he that hath meat, let him do likewise" (Luke 3:11).

To the tax collectors John said, "Exact no more than that which is appointed you" (Luke 3:13).

John said to the soldiers, "Do violence to no man, neither accuse any falsely; and be content with your wages" (Luke 3:14).

It is remarkable that John the Baptist counseled none of these to leave their present situation. Rather, he told them how to grow *in* the situation where they found themselves.

What is there around us to do? Is there any unfinished business? Have we started projects we have not finished? Are we humble enough to do with a smile those things thought by others to be beneath them?

Is there a Sunday school class that needs a teacher? A bus that needs a driver? A lonely person we could visit? A floor that we could clean?

The "diamonds" of opportunity are in our back yard.

Get your priorities straight. As he listed the requirements for the highest spiritual office held by a man—that of a bishop—Paul emphasized a man's relationship with his wife and children (I Timothy 3:1-7).

A great deal of frustration and spiritual "burnout" can be traced to misplaced priorities. While many place "ministry" at the top of the list, the Scriptures show ministry growing out of one's personal relationship with God and with his wife and children. A man's priorities should be arranged like this:

• My personal relationship with God. This is not one's "ministry," whether that of a pastor, evangelist, teacher, Sunday school superintendent, or whatever else one may be involved in. There is a great deal of difference between a person's personal relationship with God and the work he does "for" God.

As it has been said, some are so involved in the work of God that they neglect the God of the work.

A person's personal relationship with God involves this time spent with God around His Word and in prayer. This is not time spent preparing sermons or Sunday school lessons, but time spent communing with one's closest Friend.

• My relationship with my wife. After a man's relationship with God, his next priority, assuming that he is married, must be developing his relationship with his wife to its fullest potential.

This will take care, thoughtfulness, and creative thinking. A husband has the responsibility to help his wife assess her personal desires and abilities and to rise to her fullest potential. This is seen in the fact that the husband is to love his wife as Christ loved the church (Ephesians 5:23-33).

A Christian man must focus his human affection on his own wife (Proverbs 5:15-23). He is to honor his wife and to learn as much as possible about how to be a loving husband (I Peter 3:7).

- My relationship with my children. Children are a gift from God (Psalm 127:3-5). They must never be viewed as a hindrance to God's work, or as being "in the way." God's will for a man never involves the neglect of his children. Anyone who thinks that in order to do the will of God he must forsake his children is simply deceived, regardless of the stories of the accomplishments of those who may have done so. Only God knows what such people *could* have done if they had fulfilled their God-given responsibility toward their children.

A father is to teach his children about the heavenly Father by the way he relates to his children. He is to be an example before them, teaching and encouraging them in the ways of the Lord.

- Ministry for Christ. Put by many at the top of the list, ministry for Christ finds its proper place after a person's relationship to God, wife, and children. The man who attains excellence in his personal relationship with God, his wife, and his children, will have a powerful, effective ministry, whatever God has called him to do. Otherwise, a man may have a personal ministry, but it will never reach its fullest potential.

Be yourself. One of the greatest hindrances to fulfilling one's potential is the vain attempt to be another person.

There are no clones in the church. The New Testament recognizes the diversities of gifts, personalities, and viewpoints and makes allowances for them within the framework of Christianity.

One of the best examples of this is Romans 14 which, while dealing with differences of opinion on non-essential issues, contains such striking statements as the following:

"Let every man be fully persuaded in his own mind" (verse 5).

"Happy is he that condemneth not himself in that thing which he alloweth" (verse 22).

While the purpose of this chapter is not to comment on Romans 14, these statements do indicate the individuality of each person. And Paul made no attempt to force each person into the same mold. Indeed, he did just the opposite. He commanded mutual appreciation from those who had diverse points of view.

Rather than trying to be someone else, a man must assess his own situation and gifts and be the best he can be. He should realize that his uniqueness is the frame within which he must display the person of Christ.

The Jewish Rabbi Rashi is reported to have said that when he stood before God he was not afraid God would ask, "Rashi, why weren't you Abraham?" or "Rashi, why weren't you Moses?" Rather, he said he was afraid God would ask him, "Rashi, why weren't you Rashi?"

Romans 14:12 declares, "So then every one of us shall give account of himself to God." God will not ask us why we were not someone else. If anything, He will ask why we failed to be ourselves, to fulfill the unique potential He had given us.

Stretch. A well-known cliché suggests that some people have twenty years' experience, while others have one year's experience twenty times. A great deal of frustration is bred in those who spend their entire lives tramping around in the same circle.

It is never too late for a person to stretch, to grow, to learn something new, to take on a new challenge. Life is made exciting by the pushing back of new frontiers, the exploration of fresh territory.

A Christian should not allow himself to be trapped in the rut of mediocrity. He can read a book, take a class, learn a new skill. By all means we should grow in our experiences with Jesus Christ.

God has us where we are for a purpose. Just as Joshua of old was being prepared by God for greater things while he assisted Moses, so our greatest opportunity may be just around the corner, pending our performance in our present situation. (See Joshua 1; 2.)

We should do the best we possibly can where we are. We do not need to kill time; rather we can look for ways to improve our performance on the job, our relationship with our wife and children, our personal time with God, and our service in His work.

Looking around us at the opportunities God has given us, we can step through the open doors. There is truth to the maxim that success comes to those who "find a need and fill it." There are certainly many needs around each of us. There is no need to look far.

What we begin, we need to finish. We should stay with our projects until they are completed.

And we need to make up our mind to enjoy what we are doing. We must not let ourselves fall for the lie that the grass on the other side of the fence is greener. Instead, we need to go to work on the field God has given us to bring it up to its fullest potential.

Test Your Knowledge

1. How do the metaphors of the church as a human body and as a temple illustrate individuality?

2. What three lessons may be drawn from I Corinthians 7:17-24?

3. What is your definition of success?

4. How would you set priorities when considering God, your personal ministry, and your family?

5. What are the four things a person can do to bloom where he is planted? What other things can you think of?

Apply Your Knowledge

Since priorities have a way of being determined by time, for one week keep a careful recording of how you spend every moment of each day. How much time do you spend sleeping? Reading your Bible? Praying? Getting ready for work? Working? With your wife? Your children? At church? In ministry?

After keeping record of your schedule for one week, examine it carefully and set new priorities where they should be. While you may not be able to do much about the hours you spend sleeping or working, you can probably adjust the time you allot for the other things in your life.

Write down at least one thing you will do differently during the coming week during your personal devotions, with your wife, with your children, on the job, and in your ministry for Jesus Christ.

Expand Your Knowledge

Consider these resources:

J. A. Robinson, *St. Paul's Epistle to the Ephesians,* quoted in Robert L. Saucy, *The Church in God's Program* (Chicago, IL: Moody Press, 1971), 36.

Russell H. Conwell, *Acres of Diamonds* (Old Tappan, NJ: Fleming H. Revell Company, 1960).

As you read *Acres of Diamonds,* ask yourself, "What are the diamonds God has put around me?"